HIGH
SOCIETY

Other humorous quotation books by Prion:

Des MacHale
Wit
Wit Hits The Spot
Wit On Target
Wit – The Last Laugh
Wit Rides Again

Aubrey Malone
The Cynic's Dictionary

Michelle Lovric
Women's Wicked Wit

Rosemarie Jarski
Hollywood Wit

Look out for:

Michael Powell
Funny Money

HIGH SOCIETY

Michael Powell

PRION

First published 2002 in Great Britain by
Prion Books Limited
Imperial Works, Perren Street
London NW5 3ED
www.prionbooks.com

ISBN 1-85375-480-3

Cover design by Julie Patmore

Printed and bound in Great Britain
by Creative Print & Design Limited, South Wales

CONTENTS

A

B

C

D

A TOAST

Here's to living single and drinking double!
May you live all the years of your life.

Jonathan Swift

Enjoy yourself. It's later than you think.

Chinese proverb

Let us have wine and women, mirth and
laughter,
Sermons and soda-water the day after.

Lord Byron, 'Don Juan'

May the Lord keep you in His hand
And never close His fist too tight.

Irish blessing

Here's to girls and gunpowder!

Gregory Peck

May you have the hindsight to know where you've been, the foresight to know where you're going and the insight to know when you're going too far.

Irish toast

To get the full value of joy you must have someone to divide it with.

Mark Twain

May bad fortune follow you all your days
And never catch up with you.

Anon

May the grass grow long on the road to hell for want of use.

Irish toast

To temperance ... in moderation.

Lem Motlow

Give me wine to wash me clean
From the weather-stains of care.

Ralph Waldo Emerson

Here's looking at you, kid.

'Rick', *Casablanca*

I drink to your charm, your beauty and your
brains: which gives you a rough idea of how
hard up I am for a drink.

Groucho Marx

May you be in heaven half an hour before the
devil knows you're dead.

Irish toast

Once in a restaurant I made a toast to her…The
best woman a man ever had. The waiter joined
me.

Rodney Dangerfield

May you live as long as you want, and never want as long as you live.

Irish toast

May the people who dance on your grave get cramps in their legs.

Yiddish toast

We drink one another's health and spoil our own.

Jerome K. Jerome, *Idle Thoughts of an Idle Fellow*

May you live to be a hundred years, with one extra year to repent.

Irish toast

ADDICTION

If you wonder if you're an addict, you probably are.

Anon

Why is it drug addicts and computer aficionados are both called users?

Clifford Stoll

It is not I who become addicted, it is my body.

Jean Cocteau

All sin tends to be addictive, and the terminal point of addiction is what is called damnation.

W. H. Auden

I'm not a drug addict. I take drugs to feel normal, to get level. I regulate my intake very precisely.

'Eugene Sands', *Playing God*

The whole LSD, STP, marijuana, heroin, hashish, prescription cough medicine crowd suffers from the 'Watchtower' itch: you gotta be with us, man, or you're out, you're dead. This pitch is a continual and seeming MUST with those who use the stuff. It's no wonder they keep getting busted.

Charles Bukowski

There is only one reason why men become addicted to drugs: they are weak men. Only strong men are cured, and they cure themselves.

Martin H. Fischer

ALCOHOL

Sophistication is a light veneer easily dissolved in alcohol.

Anon

Reality is impossible to take neat; we must dilute it with alcohol.

Peter De Vries

If you give a chemist a bottle of alcohol, we can make anything you want.

Robert Heinlein

Alcohol is the devil's urine.

Charlie Sheen

Two great European narcotics: alcohol and Christianity.

Friedrich Nietzsche

7

Our national drug is alcohol. We tend to regard the use of any other drug with special horror. Anyone given over to these alien vices deserves the complete ruin of his mind and body. People believe what they want to believe without regard for the facts.

William S. Burroughs

I took a drink of water recently, and I want to tell you something. Water is OK to bathe in or shave in, but as a beverage it's a 100 per cent failure.

Hamper MacBee

Alcohol is my way of life, and I aim to keep it.

Homer Simpson

Alcohol is barren. The words a man speaks in the night of drunkenness fade like the darkness itself at the coming of day.

Marguerite Duras

Alcohol is the anaesthesia by which we endure the operation of life.

George Bernard Shaw

To alcohol! The cause of – and solution to – all of life's problems.

Homer Simpson

I have taken more out of alcohol than alcohol has taken out of me.

Sir Winston Churchill

Tobacco and alcohol, delicious fathers of abiding friendships and fertile reveries.

Luis Buñuel

Alcohol is a very necessary article ... it enables Parliament to do things at eleven that no sane person would do at eleven in the morning.

George Bernard Shaw

With alcohol there can be no change, except in
your liver.

Michael Bradley

No power on earth or above the bottomless pit
has such influence to terrorise and make
cowards of men as the liquor power. Satan could
not have fallen on a more potent instrument
with which to thrall the world. Alcohol is king!

Eliza Stewart, American temperance leader

Using one of the world's largest radio telescopes,
British scientists have analyzed an interstellar
gas cloud and calculated that it contains enough
alcohol to make 400 trillion trillion pints of
beer...

New York Times, 30 May, 1995

Alcohol is a good preservative for everything but
brains.

Mary Pettibone Poole

Alcohol produces ten times the amount of suffering that arsenic does. The latter destroys life; a few brief hours of agony, and its work is done; but the agony caused by alcohol, extending over months to years, torments its victim with more than tenfold cruelty.

The Temperance Handbook

Of course power tools and alcohol don't mix. Everyone knows power tools aren't soluble in alcohol.

Crazy Nigel

Alcohol is necessary for a man so that he can have a good opinion of himself, undisturbed by the facts.

Finley Peter Dunne

Substituting God for alcohol or any other drug is indeed a swapping of dependencies. But last I looked, God didn't eat your liver.

Judex

I hung around with a group of medical students. They were lunatics. They had this neat surgical alcohol, which we used to mix with orange juice. It was rocket fuel. It was insane… It scares me thinking about it now.

Chris Tarrant (talking about his time at University)

No other human being, no woman, no poem or music, book or painting can replace alcohol in its power to give man the illusion of real creation.

Marguerite Duras

Alcohol may be man's worst enemy. But the Bible says love your enemy.

Anon

When I sell liquor, it's called bootlegging; when my patrons serve it on silver trays on Lake Shore Drive, it's called hospitality.

Al Capone

Alcohol rewards its followers with the gift of mediocrity while offering the illusion of greatness.

Michael Bradley

Reality is a delusion created by an alcohol deficiency.

Anon

Maybe alcohol picks you up a little bit, but it sure lets you down in a hurry.

Betty Ford

ALCOHOLISM

I may have another drunk in me, but do I have another recovery?

Alcoholics Anonymous

Sure I had a drinking problem, but I looked at it more as a drinking opportunity.

Anon

I don't suffer from alcoholism. I enjoy every minute of it.

Anon

MAJOR STRASSER: What is your nationality?
RICK: I'm a drunkard.
CAPT. RENAULT: That makes Rick a citizen of the world.

Casablanca

Why are there more old drunks than old doctors?

Anon

Alcoholism is the only disease that tries to convince you that you don't have it.

Alcoholics Anonymous

The last mosquito that bit me had to book into the Betty Ford clinic.

'Patsy', *Absolutely Fabulous*

Alcoholism isn't a spectator sport. Eventually the whole family gets to play.

Joyce Rebeta-Burditt

An alcoholic is someone whose feet are firmly planted in thin air.

Anon

I demand to have some booze!

'Withnail', *Withnail and I*

I distrust a man who says 'when'. If he's got to be careful not to drink too much, it's because he's not to be trusted when he does.

'Sidney Greenstreet', *The Maltese Falcon*

I must have a drink by eleven, it's a deed that must be done. If I can't have a drink by eleven, I must have eleven by one.

Anon

Alcoholism is a search for a common language, or at least, it is a compensation for a language that has been lost.

Octavio Paz

He was vaguely aware that he drank to forget. The problem was that he could no longer remember what he was forgetting, so in the end he just drank to forget drinking.

Terry Pratchett, *Guards! Guards!*

I drink too much. The last time I gave a urine sample it had an olive in it.

Rodney Dangerfield

I'm not a heavy drinker: I can sometimes go for hours without touching a drop.

Noel Coward

The alcoholic's mind is like a bad neighbour-hood: Don't go there alone.

Anon

I can't die until the government finds a safe place to bury my liver.

Phil Harris

There's no one too dumb for this program, but it's possible to be too smart.

Alcoholics Anonymous

First you take a drink, then the drink takes a drink, then the drink takes you.

F. Scott Fitzgerald

If drinking is interfering with your work, you're probably a heavy drinker. If work is interfering with your drinking, you're probably an alcoholic.

Anon

You can't drown yourself in drink: I've tried, you float.

John Barrymore

A drunk is a sick human being trying to get well, not a bad one trying to be good.

Alcoholics Anonymous

It's a wonderful thing, the DTs. You can travel the world in a couple of hours. You see some mighty funny and curious things that come in assorted colours.

W. C. Fields

An alcoholic has been lightly defined as a man who drinks more than his own doctor.

Alvan L. Barach

My father? My father left when I was quite young. Well actually, he was asked to leave. He had trouble metabolising alcohol.

George Carlin

The definition of an alcoholic: an egomaniac with an inferiority complex.

Anon

You're a drunk, a tramp and an unfit mother!

'J. R. Ewing', *Dallas*

Alcohol is like love. The first kiss is magic, the second is intimate, the third is routine. After that you take the girl's clothes off.

Raymond Chandler

My make-up wasn't smeared, I wasn't dishevelled, I behaved politely, and I never finished off a bottle, so how could I be alcoholic?

Betty Ford

Unrecognised alcoholism is the ruling pathology among writers and intellectuals.

Diane Trilling

There's nothing worse than an introspective drunk.

Tom Sharpe

Alcoholism is the only disease that tells you you're all right.

Alcoholics Anonymous

The person with the most sobriety at a meeting is the one who got up earliest that morning.

Alcoholics Anonymous

BEER

God, I'd give anything for a drink. I'd give my god-damned soul for just a glass of beer!

'Jack Torrance', *The Shining*

Beer does not make you fat. It makes you lean … against bars, poles and tables.

Anon

Adhere to *Schweinheitsgebot*. Don't put anything in your beer that a pig wouldn't eat.

David Geary

Put it back in the horse!

H. Allen Smith (on American beer)

It's better to have beer in hand than gas in tank.

Anon

Boston is a city with champagne tastes and beer pocketbooks.

Alan Friedberg

The best beer in the world is the open bottle in your hand!

Danny Jansen

Mike Hammer drinks beer, not cognac, because I can't spell cognac.

Mickey Spillane

They proceeded with the speed of rockets to the northeast corner of the universe, which George perceived to be shaped exactly like a pint of beer, in which the nebulae were the ascending bubbles.

John Collier, *The Devil, George, and Rosie*

The hardest part of brewing beer is selling it.

Carol Stoudt

A good beer is one that sells! You may think it sucks but if the market embraces it, so be it. Now a great beer or world class beer is another matter.

Jim Busch

I liked the taste of beer, its live, white lather, its brass-bright depths, the sudden world through the wet brown walls of the glass ... the foam on the corners.

Dylan Thomas, *Portrait of the Artist as a Young Dog*

I am the first man south of the Mason-Dixon line to brew a drinkable home-brew.

H. L. Mencken

Give a man a beer, waste an hour. Teach a man to brew, and waste a lifetime!

Bill Owen, *American Brewer Magazine*

Beer isn't just beer ... beer needs a home.

Die Welt, 1976

Light beer is an invention of the Prince of Darkness.

Inspector Morse

I would rather commit adultery than drink a glass of beer.

Lady Astor

Man's way to God is with beer in hand.

Koffyar tribal wisdom, Nigeria

Beer. Helping ugly people have sex since 1862.

Anon

Beer drinking doesn't do half the harm of lovemaking.

Eden Philpotts, *The Farmer's Wife*

A mouth of a perfectly happy man is filled with beer.

Ancient Egyptian proverb, 2200BC

I like beer. On occasion, I will even drink beer to celebrate a major event such as the fall of communism or the fact that the refrigerator is still working.

Dave Barry

The heart which grief hath cankered
Hath one unfailing remedy – the Tankard.

Charles Stuart Calverley

Beer by Christmas would be the most welcome news the American people could have since the depression began.

William Randolph Hearst

Beer! my father would bawl whenever some elder dared to chide his tippling. Beer is my food! To maintain his strength he seldom drank less than four quarts a day.

Robert Roberts

For a quart of Ale is a dish for a King.

William Shakespeare, *A Winter's Tale*

Quaintest thoughts, queerest fancies come to life and fade away. What care I how time advances; I am drinking ale today.

Edgar Allan Poe, 'Lines on Ale'

Good ale will make a cat speak.

Old English proverb

Beer makes you feel the way you ought to feel without beer.

Henry Lawson

The best beer is where priests go to drink.

Anon

History flows forward on rivers of beer.

Anon

OK, last one to kill a bad guy buys the beer.

'Major Don West', *Lost in Space*

It's beer o'clock, and I'm buying.

'Teddy', *Memento*

So stay at home and drink your beer and let the neighbours vote.

William Butler Yeats, 'The Old Stone Cross'

There will always be beer cans rolling on the floor of your car when the boss asks for a ride home from the office.

1st Law of Work

Wherever people drink, you can remain,
Evil beings do never a tankard drain.

Anon

You don't buy beer. You rent it.

Archie Bunker

I work until beer o'clock.

Stephen King

When I heated my home with oil, I used an average of 800 gallons a year. I have found that I can keep comfortably warm for an entire winter with slightly over half that quantity of beer.

Dave Barry

All other nations are drinking Ray Charles beer and we are drinking Barry Manilow.

Dave Barry

A beer is to be sipped, savoured and fully respected.

The Belhaven Brewery

Fermentation and civilisation are inseparable.

John Ciardi

I would propose that the government launch a
$17 billion war on light beer.

Dave Barry

To some it's a six-pack. To me it's a support
group.

Anon

Give me a woman who loves beer and I will
conquer the world.

Kaiser Wilhelm

If God had intended us to drink beer, he would
have given us stomachs.

David Daye

People who drink light beer don't like the taste
of beer; they just like to pee a lot.

Capital Brewery

Draft beer, not people.

Anon

No soldier can fight unless he is properly fed on beef and beer.

John Churchill, 1st Duke of Marlborough

It is mighty difficult to get drunk on 2.75 per cent beer.

Herbert Hoover

Beer is proof that God loves us and wants us to be happy.

Benjamin Franklin

The best way to die is sit under a tree, eat lots of bologna and salami, drink a case of beer, then blow up.

Art Donovan

Remember: 'I' before 'E', except in Budweiser.

Anon

Now son, you don't want to drink beer. That's for daddies, and kids with fake IDs.

Homer Simpson

Sometimes when I reflect back on all the beer I drink I feel ashamed. Then I look into the glass and think about the workers in the brewery and all of their hopes and dreams. If I didn't drink this beer, they might be out of work and their dreams would be shattered. Then I say to myself, 'It is better that I drink this beer and let their dreams come true than be selfish and worry about my liver.'

Jack Handy

You can't be a real country unless you have a beer and an airline – it helps if you have some kind of a football team, or some nuclear weapons, but at the very least you need a beer.

Frank Zappa

Religions change; beer and wine remain.

Hervey Allen

Not all chemicals are bad. Without chemicals such as hydrogen and oxygen, for example, there would be no way to make water, a vital ingredient in beer.

Dave Barry

Marriage is based on the theory that when man discovers a brand of beer exactly to his taste he should at once throw up his job and go work in the brewery.

George Jean Nathan

I'm only a beer teetotaller, not a champagne teetotaller. I don't like beer.

George Bernard Shaw

What two ideas are more inseparable than beer and Britannia?

Sydney Smith

Beer is the reason we get up each afternoon.

Ray McNeill

Beer, if drunk with moderation, softens the temper, cheers the spirit and promotes health.

Thomas Jefferson

They can have my beer when they pry it out of my cold, dead hand.

Ben Schwalb

Beer is the Danish national drink, and the Danish national weakness is another beer.

Clementine Paddleford

The government will fall that raises the price of beer.

Czech proverb

Life isn't all beer and skittles, but beer and skittles, or something better of the same sort, must form a good part of every Englishman's education.

Thomas Hughes

They who drink beer will think beer.

Washington Irving

Gin for executions, beer for birthdays, wine for weddings.

P. J. Wolfson

One of the few moments of happiness a man knows in Australia is that moment of meeting the eyes of another man over the tops of two beer glasses.

Bruce Chatwin

Where does one not find that bland degeneration which beer produces in the spirit?

Friedrich Nietzsche

Beer – helping white people dance since 1837.

Anon

Froth is not beer.

Dutch proverb

Your beer drinker tends to be a straightforward, decent, friendly, down-to-earth person, whereas your serious wine fancier tends to be an insufferable snot.

Dave Barry

I'm only here to do two things, drink some beer and kick some ass. Looks like we're almost out of beer.

Dazed and Confused

When I die bury me deep with a six-pack of beer between my feet, a fifth of liquor and a bottle of rum. I'll raise hell to kingdom come.

Chris Barton

Men are nicotine-soaked, beer-besmirched, whisky-greased, red-eyed devils.

Carry Nation, US social reformer

I'd offer you a beer, but I've only got six cans.

'Terry Collier', *The Likely Lads*

When the bee comes to your house, let her have beer; you may want to visit the bee's house some day.

Congolese proverb

Englishmen are like their own beer: Frothy on top, dregs on the bottom, the middle excellent.

Voltaire

Give an Irishman lager for a month and he's a dead man. An Irishman's stomach is lined with copper, and the beer corrodes it. But whisky polishes the copper and is the saving of him.

Mark Twain

I'm eleven hundred and twenty years old! Just gimme a frickin' beer!

'Anya Emerson', *Buffy the Vampire Slayer*

We brewers don't make beer, we just get all the ingredients together and the beer makes itself.

Fritz Maytag, President, Anchor Brewing

If I saved all the money I've spent on beer, I'd spend it on beer.

Anon

Where the beer is brewed, life is good; where the beer is drunk, life is even better!

Sarah Lewis

Brewers enjoy working to make beer as much as drinking beer instead of working.

Harold Rudolph

Do not cease to drink beer, to eat, to intoxicate thyself, to make love, and celebrate the good days.

Ancient Egyptian proverb

This beer is good for you. This is draft beer. Stick with the beer. Let's go and beat this guy up and come back and drink some more beer.

Ernest Hemingway, *To Have and Have Not*

Fermentation may have been a greater discovery than fire.

David Rains Wallace

If you play for England you don't need to drink wine or beer with your meals. We are together to play football, not for anything else.

Sven-Goran Eriksson

I recommend bread, meat, vegetables and beer.

Sophocles

The perfect life: A clean warm beach, a hot woman, sweet crabs, a cold Guinness, and the money to enjoy it!

Lenny Hoben

Aww there's only one beer left and it's Bart's!

Homer Simpson

I'm allergic to grass. Hey, it could be worse. I could be allergic to beer.

Greg Norman

From man's sweat and God's love, beer came into the world.

Saint Arnold of Metz, Patron Saint of Brewers

You can only drink 30 or 40 glasses of beer a day, no matter how rich you are.

Colonel Adolphus Busch

Keep your libraries, your penal institutions, your insane asylums … give me beer. You think man needs rule, he needs beer. The world does not need morals, it needs beer… The souls of men have been fed with indigestibles, but the soul could make use of beer.

Henry Miller, *Make Beer For Man*

How can you waste beer like that! Don't you realise there are sober children in Africa!

Anon

A little bit of beer is divine medicine.

Paracelsus

Strong beer, a liquor extracted with very little art from wheat or barley, and corrupted (as it is strongly expressed by Tacitus) into a certain semblance of wine, was sufficient for the gross purposes of German debauchery.

Edward Gibbon

I'm an old-fashioned guy ... I want to be an old man with a beer belly sitting on a porch, looking at a lake or something.

Johnny Depp

I'm a big fan of beer ads. They're extremely clever and entertaining. I love the jingles. I could watch beer ads all night. Just don't ask me to drink the beer.

Jim Koch

Once you begin to learn about the nature of beer bubbles, you will never again look at a glass of beer in quite the same way.

Neil Shafer and Richard Zare (Stanford University chemists)

Never wear button-fly jeans to a beer dinner.

Anon

There are 6,999 drops of beer in a standard 12-ounce bottle.

Canadian Ace Brewing Company

I would like a great lake of beer for the King of Kings. I would like to be watching Heaven's family drinking it through all eternity.

Medieval Irish poem

And so they've defeated us year after year,
But sure there was plenty of whisky and beer.

Song satirising the Democratic Party (c.1880)

Beer is an improvement on water itself.

Grant Johnson

From the boundaries of heaven and earth, by grace of Saint Arnold, and through human skill was born beer, a gift of the gods.

Written on the wall of the Confederation of Belgian Brewers in Brussels' Grand Place

I feel wonderful, drinking beer in a blissful mood, with joy in my heart and a happy liver.

Sumerian inscription c.3000BC

BRANDY

Glass of brandy and water! That is the current but not the appropriate name: ask for a glass of liquid fire and distilled damnation.

Robert Hall

42

BRANDY, *n.* A cordial composed of one part thunder-and-lightning, one part remorse, two parts bloody murder, one part death-hell-and-the-grave and four parts clarified Satan. Dose, a headful all the time. Brandy is said by Dr. Johnson to be the drink of heroes. Only a hero will venture to drink it.

Ambrose Bierce, *The Devil's Dictionary*

Claret is the liquor for boys; port for men; but he who aspires to be a hero must drink brandy.

Samuel Johnson

NORRIS: How do you like your brandy, sir?
PHILIP MARLOWE: In a glass.

The Big Sleep

Harris, I am not well; pray get me a glass of brandy.

George IV, on first seeing Caroline of Brunswick, his future wife

An American monkey, an Ateles, after getting drunk on brandy, would never touch it again, and thus was wiser than many men. These trifling facts prove how similar the nerves of taste must be in monkeys and man, and how similarly their whole nervous system is affected.

Charles Darwin, *The Descent of Man*

Have ready a bottle of brandy, because I always feel like drinking that heroic drink when we talk ontological heroics together.

Herman Melville to Nathaniel Hawthorne, 29 June 1851

CHAMPAGNE

I like champagne because it always tastes as though my foot's asleep.

Art Buchwald

Fighting is like champagne. It goes to the heads of cowards as quickly as of heroes. Any fool can be brave on a battle field when it's be brave or else be killed.

Margaret Mitchell, *Gone with the Wind*

The House of Lords is like a glass of champagne that has stood for five days.

Clement Attlee

A woman should never be seen eating or drinking, unless it be lobster salad and Champagne, the only true feminine and becoming viands.

Lord Byron

Champagne is the only wine that enhances a woman's beauty.

Madame de Pompadour

I'll stick with gin. Champagne is just ginger ale that knows somebody.

'Hawkeye', *M.A.S.H.*

I drink it when I'm happy and when I'm sad. Sometimes, I drink it when I'm alone. When I have company I consider it obligatory. I trifle with it if I'm not hungry and drink it if I am; Otherwise I never touch it – unless I'm thirsty.

Madame Bollinger

Too much of anything is bad, but too much Champagne is just right.

Mark Twain

Champagne is the wine of civilisation and the oil of government.

Talleyrand

One holds a bottle of red wine by the neck, a woman by the waist, and a bottle of Champagne by the derrière.

Anon

Champagne offers a minimum of alcohol and a maximum of companionship.

David Niven

Three are the things I shall never attain: envy, contentment, and sufficient champagne.

Dorothy Parker, 'Inventory'

Champagne makes you feel like it's Sunday and better days are just around the corner.

Marlene Dietrich

Gentlemen, in the little moment that remains to us between the crisis and the catastrophe, we may as well drink a glass of Champagne.

Paul Claudel

My dear girl, there are some things that just aren't done, such as drinking Dom Perignon '53 above the temperature of 38 degrees Fahrenheit. That's just as bad as listening to the Beatles without earmuffs!

Ian Fleming, *Goldfinger*

Come, I am tasting the stars!

Dom Pérignon

Here's to champagne, the drink divine, that makes us forget all our troubles;
It's made of a dollar's worth of wine, and three dollars worth of bubbles.

Anon

It had the taste of an apple peeled with a steel knife.

Aldous Huxley (assessing a Roederer 1916 champagne)

He who doesn't risk never gets to drink champagne.

Russian proverb

In victory, you deserve champagne, in defeat, you need it.

Napoleon Bonaparte

My only regret in life is that I did not drink more champagne.

John Maynard Keynes

Champagne and potato chips! This is a wonderful party!

'The Girl', *The Seven Year Itch*

I'll never be able to afford it so I better buy it now.

Andrew Scott

I didn't know they made champagne in Idaho.

'Stephanie', *Cactus Flower*

Meeting Franklin Roosevelt was like opening your first bottle of champagne; knowing him was like drinking it.

Sir Winston Churchill

Champagne's funny stuff. I'm used to whisky. Whisky's a slap on the back and champagne's heavy mist before my eyes.

'Macauley Connor', *Philadelphia Story*

Give the servants some champagne. This [wine] is wasted on them.

Baron Frankenstein, *Frankenstein*

I would offer you a glass of champagne, but it's bad for you in small doses.

Jason King

Great love affairs start with champagne and end with tisane.

Honoré de Balzac

Champagne, if you are seeking the truth, is better than a lie detector. It encourages a man to be expansive, even reckless, while lie detectors are only a challenge to tell lies successfully.

Graham Greene

Remember gentlemen, it's not just France we are fighting for, it's champagne!

Sir Winston Churchill

There comes a time in every woman's life when
the only thing that helps is a glass of champagne.

Bette Davis

Some people wanted champagne and caviar
when they should have had beer and hot dogs.

Dwight D. Eisenhower

I really like only champagne. The trouble is, it
gives you permanently bad breath.

Elizabeth Taylor

CHOCOLATE

Since both its [Switzerland's] national products,
snow and chocolate, melt, the cuckoo clock was
invented solely in order to give tourists something solid to remember it by.

Alan Coren, *The Sanity Inspector*

Researchers have discovered that chocolate produces some of the same reactions in the brain as marijuana. The researchers also discovered other similarities between the two, but can't remember what they are.

Mat Lauer

What you see before you, my friend, is the result of a lifetime of chocolate.

Katharine Hepburn

Once in a while I say, 'Go for it' and I eat chocolate.

Claudia Schiffer

It's not that chocolates are a substitute for love. Love is a substitute for chocolate. Chocolate is, let's face it, far more reliable than a man.

Miranda Ingram

If you get melted chocolate all over your hands, you're eating it too slowly.

Anon

Self-discipline implies some unpleasant things to me, including staying away from chocolate and keeping my hands out of women's pants.

Oleg Kiselev

It has been shown as proof positive that carefully prepared chocolate is as healthful a food as it is pleasant; that it is nourishing and easily digested . . . that it is above all helpful to people who must do a great deal of mental work.

Anthelme Brillat-Savarin

Strength is the capacity to break a chocolate bar into four pieces with your bare hands – and then eat just one of the pieces.

Judith Viorst

Chocolate is no ordinary food. It is not something you can take or leave, something you like only moderately. You don't like chocolate. You don't even love chocolate. Chocolate is something you have an affair with.

Geneen Roth

CIGARS

What this country needs is a really good 5-cent cigar.

Thomas R. Marshall

Follow the cigar smoke, find the fat man there.

Native American Indian proverb

I must point out that my rule of life prescribed as an absolutely sacred rite smoking cigars and also the drinking of alcohol before, after, and if need be during all meals and in the intervals between them.

Sir Winston Churchill

A woman is only a woman,
but a good cigar is a smoke.

Rudyard Kipling

If I cannot smoke cigars in Heaven, I shall not go.

Mark Twain

Sometimes a cigar is just a cigar.

Sigmund Freud

A woman is an occasional pleasure but a cigar is always a smoke.

Groucho Marx

Living in Hollywood is like living in a lit cigar butt.

Phyllis Diller

Daydreaming while smoking cigars can be a fire hazard. It can be as dangerous as drugs and booze unless you know what you're doing. If you know what you're doing, it can be as safe as walking down the street.

Kinky Friedman

Is it true that you smoke eight to ten cigars a
day?
That's true.
Is it true that you drink five martinis a day?
That's true.
Is it true that you still surround yourself with
beautiful young women?
That's true.
What does your doctor say about all of this?
My doctor is dead.

George Burns

Pull out a Monte Cristo at a dinner party and
the political liberal turns into the nicotine fascist.

Martyn Harris

Every cigar goes up in smoke.

Brazilian proverb

I don't trust air I can't see.

'Captain Ramsey', *Crimson Tide*

The most futile and disastrous day seems well
spent when it is reviewed through the blue,
fragrant smoke of a Havana cigar.

Evelyn Waugh

He who has money smokes cigars,
But he who has no money smokes paper.

Spanish proverb

Do not ask me to describe the charms of reverie,
or the contemplative ecstasy into which the
smoke of our cigar plunges us.

Jules Sandeau

To smoke is human; to smoke cigars is divine.

Anon

I smoke in moderation, only one cigar at a time.

Mark Twain

A good cigar is as great a comfort to a man as a good cry to a woman.

E. G. Bulwer-Lytton

After a truly good meal, an outstanding cigar is still the most satisfying after-dinner activity that doesn't involve two human beings.

Brad Shaw

A cigar has a fire at one end and a fool at the other.

Horace Greely

The cigar numbs sorrow and fills the solitary hours with a million gracious images.

George Sand

If your wife doesn't like the aroma of your cigar, change your wife.

Zino Davidoff

Given the choice between a woman and a cigar,
I will always choose the cigar.

Groucho Marx

To know how to smoke is to recover certain
forgotten rhythms, to re-establish communication
with the self.

Zino Davidoff

If you kiss a cigar, it will kiss you back. If you
treat it like a dog, it will turn around and bite
you.

George Brightman

If the birth of a genius resembles that of an
idiot, the end of a Havana Corona resembles
that of a 5-cent cigar.

Sacha Guitry

A good Cuban cigar closes the door to the
vulgarities of the world.

Franz Liszt

A good cigar is like tasting a good wine: you smell it, you taste it, you look at it, you feel it – you can even hear it. It satisfies all the senses.

Anon

A woman is just a script, but a cigar is a motion picture.

Samuel Fuller

Women are really jealous of cigars ... they regard them as a strong rival.

William Makepeace Thackeray

Only fine cigars are worth smoking and only men who smoke fine cigars are worth kissing.

Joan Collins

I promised myself that if ever I had some money that I would savour a cigar each day after lunch and dinner. This is the only resolution of my youth that I have kept, and the only realised ambition which has not brought disillusion.

W. Somerset Maugham

Asthma doesn't seem to bother me any more unless I'm around cigars or dogs. The thing that would bother me most would be a dog smoking a cigar.

Steve Allen

If I paid ten dollars for a cigar, first I'd make love to it, then I'd smoke it.

George Burns

Unlike wines, from which you can take several sips and go on to taste a hundred or more during a day, a cigar has to be smoked from beginning to end before it can be properly evaluated.

Daniel Rogov

CIGARETTES

The filter's the best part. That's where they put the heroin.

Denis Leary

Killing isn't like smoking. You can stop.

'Catherine Tramell', *Basic Instinct*

Hey, you know, I have had it with you guys and your 'cancer' and your 'emphysema' and your 'heart disease'. The bottom line is smoking is cool and you know it.

'Chandler Bing', *Friends*

I see you're smoking pot now. I suppose you think smoking illegal psychotropic substances is a good example to set for our sixteen-year-old daughter?

'Carolyn Burnham', *American Beauty*

I found some cigarettes. I found them all the way in the bottom of my pack. We're still alive 'cause we're smoking.

'Mike', *The Blair Witch Project*

Coffee-flavoured cigarettes: kill yourself twice as fast.

Anon

Do you know what smoking does to you? It
stunts your growth, it yellows your teeth and
blackens your lungs. Is that what you want? To
be a yellow toothed midget with lung cancer?

'Norman Robberson', *Cops and Robbersons*

Smokers. There's no excuse for smoking.
Smoking is the equivalent to carrying around a
salt lick, laced with a little bit of cyanide.

'Thane Furrows', *High Strung*

Yeah, studies show that smoking in the shower
reduces risk of fire by about a half.

'Will Sly', *If You Could See What I Hear*

Bless the saints, it's an ashtray! I've been
thinking of taking up smoking. This clinches it!

'Ma Kelly', *Johnny Dangerously*

Yes. Give him his cigarettes. It won't be the
nicotine that kills you, Mr Bond.

Ian Fleming, *You Only Live Twice*

Tell me, why do so many men smoke afterwards? No wonder tobacco companies get rich.

'Maria Gambrelli', *A Shot in the Dark*

Yes, I am smoking cigarettes and some of my friends have died of them, but I am not downing a quart of Scotch in fifteen minutes. Looked at that way, cigarettes are actually a health tool!

Lou Reed, *Blue in the Face*

It's a funny thing about television and cigarettes. Hardly anybody I know anymore smokes cigarettes or watches the tube. One stunts the body and one stunts the mind.

John D. MacDonald

One of the most important drug-policy issues is the level of tobacco taxes.

Mark Kleiman

Much smoking kills live men and cures dead swine.

George D. Prentice

The best way to stop smoking is to carry wet matches.

Anon

I tried to stop smoking cigarettes by telling myself I just didn't want to smoke, but I didn't believe myself.

Barbara Kelly

He drew in the smoke of his cigarette as if the soothing influence was grateful to him.

Sir Arthur Conan Doyle, *The Final Problem*

[Do you mind if I smoke?]
Certainly not – if you don't object if I'm sick.

Sir Thomas Beecham

What a blessing this smoking is! Perhaps the greatest that we owe to the discovery of America.

Arthur Helps

A custom loathsome to the eye, hateful to the nose, harmful to the brain, dangerous to the lungs, and in the black, stinking fume thereof, nearest resembling the horrible Stygian smoke of the pit that is bottomless.

King James I

Neither do thou lust after that tawney weed tobacco.

Ben Jonson, *Bartholemew Fair*

This vice brings in one hundred million francs in taxes every year. I will certainly forbid it at once – as soon as you can name a virtue that brings in as much revenue.

Napoleon III

My doctor has always told me to smoke. He even explains himself: 'Smoke, my friend. Otherwise someone else will smoke in your place.'

Erik Satie

I asked a coughing friend of mine why he doesn't stop smoking. 'In this town it wouldn't do any good,' he explained. 'I happen to be a chain breather.'

Robert Sylvester

Tobacco drieth the brain, dimmeth the sight, vitiateth the smell, hurteth the stomach, destroyeth the concoction, disturbeth the humors and spirits, corrupteth the breath, induceth a trembling of the limbs, exsiccateth the windpipe, lungs, and liver, annoyeth the milt, scorcheth the heart, and causeth the blood to be adjusted.

Tobias Venner

Please don't throw cigarettes in the toilet. It makes them sticky, wet and hard to light.

Graffiti

Smoking: Suicide on an instalment plan.

Anon

Researchers linked smoking to cancer in the 1950s. Doctors believed them in the 1960s, but it was not until journalists believed the doctors in the 1970s that the public took notice.

Richard Peto

When are people going to realise that breathing in smoke from anything that burns is not a good idea?

Duane Alan Hahn

What lovelier sight is there than that double row of white cigarettes, lined up like soldiers on parade and wrapped in silver paper? ... I love to touch the pack in my pocket, open it, savour the feel of the cigarette between my fingers, the paper on my lips, the taste of tobacco on my tongue. I love to watch the flame spurt up, love to watch it come closer and closer, filling me with its warmth.

Luis Buñuel

If children don't like to be in a smoky room, they'll leave. At some point, they [infants] begin to crawl.

Charles Harper, Chairman, R. J. Reynolds

He who lives without tobacco is not worthy to live.

Molière

Smoking is another word for self-imposed wrinkles.

Duane Alan Hahn

I phoned my dad to tell him I had stopped smoking. He called me a quitter.

Steven Pearl

Nicotine patches are great. Stick one over each eye and you can't find your fags.

Bill Hicks

But when I don't smoke I scarcely feel as if I'm living. I don't feel as if I'm living unless I'm killing myself.

Russell Hoban

There are some circles in America where it seems to be more socially acceptable to carry a hand-gun than a packet of cigarettes.

Katharine Whitehorn

Sublime tobacco! which from east to west
Cheers the tar's labour or the Turkman's rest.

Lord Byron, 'The Island'

Smokers, male and female, inject and excuse idleness in their lives every time they light a cigarette.

Colette

A cigarette is the perfect type of a perfect pleasure. It is exquisite, and it leaves one unsatisfied. What more can one want?

Oscar Wilde

I attribute the quarrelsome nature of the young men of the Middle Ages entirely to the want of the soothing weed.

Jerome K. Jerome, *Idle Thoughts of an Idle Fellow*

I see not much difference between ourselves and the Turks, save that we have foreskins and they none, that they have long dresses and we short, and that we talk much and they little. In England the vices in fashion are whoring and drinking, in Turkey, sodomy and smoking.

Lord Byron

If the devil were to offer me a resurgence of what is commonly called virility, I'd decline. 'Just keep my liver and lungs in good working order,' I'd reply, 'so I can go on drinking and smoking!'

Luis Buñuel

The sex was so good that even the neighbours had a cigarette.

Anon

For thy sake, tobacco, I would do anything but die.

Charles Lamb

I make it a rule never to smoke while I'm sleeping.

Mark Twain

Giving up smoking is the easiest thing in the world. I know because I've done it thousands of times.

Mark Twain

Smoking kills. If you're killed, you've lost a very important part of your life.

Brooke Shields (during an interview to become spokes-person for a federal anti-smoking campaign)

If there isn't a population problem, why is the government putting cancer in the cigarettes?

Anon

You can never get the smell of smoke out. Like the smell of failure in life.

John Updike, *Rabbit Redux*

Don't think of it as a cigarette ... think of it as the thing that's been missing from your hand.

'Chandler Bing', *Friends*

Odd as it sounds I really like the smell of smoke, but I don't enjoy smoking. You have any idea how hard it is to find a smoke-filled room these days?

John Dobbin

If I want to stop smoking, one method is to find a tall building and jump off. But that's kind of a high-cost solution.

Ari Rapkin

Cigarette smoking is a major cause of statistics.

Fletcher Knebel

On CBS Radio the news of his [Ed Murrow's] death, reportedly from lung cancer, was followed by a cigarette commercial.

Alexander Kendrick

Your grandchildren will likely find it incredible – or even sinful – that you burned up a gallon of gasoline to fetch a pack of cigarettes!

Dr Paul MacCready, Jr.

What torture, this life in society! Often someone is obliging enough to offer me a light, and in order to oblige him I have to fish a cigarette out of my pocket.

Karl Kraus

I'll tell you why I like the cigarette business. It costs a penny to make. Sell it for a dollar. It's addictive. And there's a fantastic brand loyalty.

Warren Buffett

I have stopped smoking now and then, for a few months at a time, but it was not on principle, it was only to show off; it was to pulverise those critics who said I was a slave to my habits and couldn't break my bonds.

Mark Twain

I kissed my first girl and smoked my first cigarette on the same day. I haven't had time for tobacco since.

Arturo Toscanini

The same people who tell us that smoking doesn't cause cancer are now telling us that advertising cigarettes doesn't cause smoking.

Ellen Goodman

Technological innovation has done great damage ... to eating habits. Food is now available in such unpleasant forms that one frequently finds smoking between courses to be an aid to digestion.

Fran Lebowitz

The modern cigarette is extremely complex. It contains everything from sugar to liquorice, chocolate, herbs and spices. There are 8,000 or more chemicals that come out when you light it and having them delivered in the right ratios is a substantial engineering feat.

Dr William Farone, Former Director of Applied Research, Philip Morris

I feel the happiest when I can light my American cigarettes with Soviet matches.

Mohammed Daud Khan, former President of Afghanistan

Tobacco has always held up Kentucky. There just aren't a lot of options. We can sell our farms and houses, but then what are we going to do?

John Fritz, tobacco farmer

If our lungs were on the outside of our bodies, none of us would smoke.

Holly 'Hotlips'

If God had intended Man to smoke, He would have set him on Fire.

Anon

Having a smoking section in a restaurant is a little like having a peeing section in a swimming pool.

Anon

Everyone seemed to treat smoking as a natural pleasure. The industry, as a result, prospered. And rightly so.

Andrew Reid, former Chairman, Imperial Tobacco

You also want to have a high degree of sexuality in the appeal … cigarettes are essentially very close to a sexual product.

Fritz Gahagan, former market research executive

Smoking is not an antisocial habit. Having sex with a black Labrador in a public toilet is an antisocial habit.

Steven Lewis

I asked her if she enjoys a cigarette after sex. She said ... No, one drag is enough.

Rodney Dangerfield

The phenomenal success of the cigarette is based on how easy it is to inhale nicotine compared to the cigar or pipe that were used in the last century. People smoke for nicotine. So you can look upon each cigarette as an injection of nicotine.

Dr William Farone, Former Director of Applied Research,
Philip Morris

If you can't send money, send tobacco.

George Washington to the Continental Congress, 1776

My dentist has bad breath... Every time he smokes he blows onion rings.

Rodney Dangerfield

Where there is idleness, weeds thrive; where there is diligence, tobacco flourishes.

Bulgarian proverb

The first thing you have to understand is that a filter is not a health device. The filter is a marketing device.

Fritz Gahagan, former market research executive

The aim of advertising is not just to sell cigarettes but to lull people's fears ... Deceptive? Of course it's deceptive. What are you going to say? Go out and buy our product, it'll kill you?

Fritz Gahagan, former market research executive

Nothing serves life and soundness of body so well, nor is so necessary as the smoke of the royal plant, tobacco.

Dr Cornelius Bontekoe (1685)

Man, the creature who knows he must die, who has dreams larger than his destiny, who is for ever working a confidence trick on himself, needs an ally. Mine has been tobacco.

J. B. Priestley

When the blazing sun tortures the peasant, it is good to the tobacco.

Bosnian proverb

Diplomacy is entirely a question of the weed. I can always settle a quarrel if I know beforehand whether the plenipotentiary smokes Cavendish, Latakia or Shag.

Lord Clarendon

There can be no doubt that smoking nowadays is largely a miserable automatic business. People use tobacco without ever taking an intelligent interest in it. They do not experiment, compare, fit the tobacco to the occasion. A man should always be pleasantly conscious of the fact that he is smoking.

J. B. Priestley

Smoking is a necessity for a person engaged in study – it stimulates the intellect and revives the spirit should lassitude set in.

Dr Beintema (1650)

Don't get upset, drink plenty of coffee, and smoke.

> Javier Pereira (allegedly 167 years old) on the secrets of longevity

If I had not smoked I should have been dead ten years ago.

> Francois Guizot

Our nation has withstood many divisions – North and South, black and white, labour and management – but I do not know if the country can survive division into smoking and non-smoking sections.

> P. J. O'Rourke

Smoking cigarettes seems to alarm peace activists much more than voting for Reagan does.

> P. J. O'Rourke

You have to work at it if you want to be a good smoker. Especially today with all the non-smoking world constantly harassing you.

Kinky Friedman

Gentlemen, you may smoke.

King Edward VII (Queen Victoria had banned smoking in court)

No woman should marry a man who does not smoke.

Robert Louis Stevenson

The believing we do something when we do nothing is the first illusion of tobacco.

Ralph Waldo Emerson

Too much experience is a dangerous thing. Pray have a cigarette. Half the pretty women in London smoke cigarettes. Personally, I prefer the other half.

Oscar Wilde, *An Ideal Husband*

Choosing to smoke is no different than choosing not to exercise or choosing to eat a hamburger instead of salad, or any of the other potentially dangerous but enjoyable things we make decisions about every day.

William Lee

Cigarette: A weed whose smoke, some say, should never be inhaled, and still more insist should never be exhaled.

Gideon Wurdz, *Foolish Dictionary*

If you seriously desire to deceive me you must change your tobacconist; for when I see the stub of a cigarette marked Bradley, Oxford Street, I know that my friend Watson is in the neighbourhood. You will see it there beside the path.

Sir Arthur Conan Doyle, *The Hound of the Baskervilles*

Let's face it, if you smoke you are going to die horribly. But smoking is cool. And it's fun. The only thing that bothers me is the passive smokers. It's outrageous. They should buy their own.

B. J. Cunningham

The cigarette… A lovely tube of delight. Look at it.

Dennis Potter (in his final televised interview with
Melvyn Bragg)

Teach the children early self-government, and teach them nothing that is wrong. If they see their father with a cigarette in his mouth – suggest to them that the habit of smoking is not nice, and that nothing but a loathsome worm naturally chews tobacco.

Mary Baker Eddy

As much as people want to call us role models, we're actors first. It's up to individuals to decide whether to smoke. I don't apologise for smoking on screen.

Winona Ryder

Cigarettes have always been about power, and most young women who smoke see themselves as sucking back a nice big dose of self-esteem.

Donna Lypchuk

Many kinds of monkeys have a strong taste for tea, coffee, and spirituous liquors: they will also, as I have myself seen, smoke tobacco with pleasure.

Charles Darwin, *Descent of Man*

To me, a cigarette is food. I live my life smoking these things, and drinking the 'black water' in this cup here.

Frank Zappa

It's big, it's clever, it's naughty, and it's dangerous. You're more or less a criminal if you smoke. Fantastic.

Alex James (lead guitarist, Blur)

We were laughing about brand names, saying how they don't reflect the real nature of the product. So we joked that there should be Pissed beer, Coronary butter – and then Death cigarettes came to us. Next morning, I woke up still laughing. Of course it's cool to smoke a cigarette called Death. It's the coolest thing imaginable.

B. J. Cunningham

The cinema has known this for a long time, too. It understands that there is no more potent symbol of romantic, hedonistic self-destruction than that of a young handsome hero or heroine drawing thoughtfully, significantly, on a coffin nail. Live fast, die young, leave a good-looking corpse.

Nigel Farndale

Kant calls 'sublime' that aesthetic experience which includes as one of its moments a negative experience, a shock, a blockage, an intimation of mortality. It is in this very strict sense that Kant gives the term that the beauty of smoking cigarettes may be considered to be sublime.

Richard Klein, *Cigarettes Are Sublime*

It is the most convenient social excuse ever invented. When confronted with someone you don't want to talk to, it's incredibly easy to excuse yourself and step outside for a moment of peace and solitude.

William Lee

Hey, all you little girls out there, sneaking out to buy cigarettes: You know why so many cigarette packages come with calendars on the back? It's so you can figure out how much time you've got left to live.

Donna Lypchuk

Smoking is the fetish of the nineties.

Dian Hanson (editor of *Leg Show*, a fetish magazine)

We don't know of one husband who battered his wife because he'd smoked too much that night. We haven't heard of any fatal car crashes caused by a driver whose 'one for the road' was a Virginia Slim. Smoking shortens lives; alcohol ruins them too.

Richard Corliss

I know that you entertain this eternal life fantasy because you've chosen not to smoke, but let me be the first to pop that bubble and bring you hurtling back to reality… You're dead too.

Bill Hicks

COCAINE

Nobody saves America by sniffing cocaine,
Jiggling yr knees blankeyed in the rain,
When it snows in yr nose you catch cold in yr
brain.

Allen Ginsberg

They shoulda called me Little Cocaine, I was
sniffing so much of the stuff! My nose got big
enough to back a diesel truck in, unload it and
drive it right out again.

Little Richard

In my day, we didn't have the cocaine, so we
went out and knocked somebody over the head
and took the money. But today, all this cocaine
and crack, it doesn't give kids a chance.

Barry White

After 20 years of taking coke, it's good to drink
Pepsi.

Mick Jagger

I took coke because I was looking for a quiet time.

Robin Williams

Tobacco shortens one's life, cocaine debases it. Nicotine alters one's habits, cocaine alters one's soul.

Anon

If addiction is judged by how long a dumb animal will sit pressing a lever to get a 'fix' of something, to its own detriment, then I would conclude that Netnews is far more addictive than cocaine.

Rob Stampfli

Taking cocaine is dropping an atomic bomb on your brain.

Arnold M. Washton

At least when I was governor, cocaine was expensive.

Jerry Brown

The irony is that as the user gets sicker, he is less able to see it. The magic of the powder is that every noseful tells you that you don't really have a problem.

Dr Joseph Pursch

The United States is like the guy at the party who gives cocaine to everybody and still nobody likes him.

Jim Samuels

Hey, I don't like cocaine . . . I just like the way it smells.

Rodney Dangerfield

Only in America would a guy invent crack. Only in America would there be a guy that cocaine wasn't good enough for.

Denis Leary

Marijuana is not a drug. I used to suck dick for coke. Now that's an addiction. You ever suck some dick for marijuana?

Anonymous cocaine addict, Half Baked

A few minutes after taking cocaine, one experiences a certain exhilaration and feeling of lightness. One feels a certain furriness on the lips and palate, followed by a feeling of warmth in the same areas... After a few minutes the actual cocaine euphoria began, introduced by repeated cooling eructation.

Sigmund Freud

Cocaine hydrochloride is very stable. It binds closely to the ink in paper currency. Hence most Americans handle cocaine every day of their lives.

Cocaine.org

No one ever feels contented after taking cocaine. They just want more.

Cocaine.org

With cocaine, one is indeed master of everything; but everything matters intensely. With
heroin, the feeling of mastery increases to such a
point that nothing matters at all.

Aleister Crowley

While there is no proof the bard delved into
narcotics, clay pipe fragments excavated from
his Stratford-upon-Avon home and of the seven-
teenth century period show conclusively that
cocaine and myristic acid – a hallucinogenic
derived from plants, including nutmeg – were
smoked in Shakespeare's England.

Ed Stoddard

See you Monday. We'll be talking about Freud
and why he did enough cocaine to kill a small
horse.

'Sean', *Good Will Hunting*

Inherited wealth is a big handicap to happiness.
It is as certain death to ambition as cocaine is to
morality.

William K. Vanderbilt

COFFEE

The average American attention span is that of a ferret on a double espresso.

Dennis Miller

Irish Coffee is the perfect breakfast because it contains all four adult food groups: fat, sugar, caffeine and alcohol.

Anon

It's easier to get people off of heroin than coffee.

Richard T. Rappolt

The fancier the name of the coffee shop, the crappier the coffee.

Vanya Cohen

Sleep is a poor substitute for caffeine.

Anon

It is the folly of too many to mistake the echo of a London coffee-house for the voice of the kingdom.

Jonathan Swift

There's too much blood in my caffeine system.

Anon

Black coffee – better than cocaine and faster.

Lothar Sticker, *Keiner liebt mich*

No, thank you. I have reached my optimum heart rate for today.

Anon

Coffee is a beverage that puts one to sleep when not drunk.

Alphonse Allais

Coffee in England is just toasted milk.

Christopher Fry

It is disgusting to notice the increase in the
quantity of coffee... Everybody is using coffee.
If possible this must be prevented. My people
must drink beer.

Frederick the Great

If this is coffee, please bring me some tea; but if
this is tea, please bring me some coffee.

Abraham Lincoln

Coffee, which makes the politician wise,
And see through all things with his half-shut
eyes.

Alexander Pope, 'The Rape of the Lock'

When I wake up in the morning, I just can't get
started until I've had that first, piping hot pot of
coffee. Oh, I've tried other enemas...

Emo Philips

Black as hell, strong as death, sweet as love.

Turkish proverb

The morning cup of coffee has an exhilaration about it which the cheering influence of the afternoon or evening cup of tea cannot be expected to reproduce.

Oliver Wendell Holmes

Coffee and cigarettes. That's like the breakfast of champions.

'Bob', *Blue in the Face*

Thank you for the coffee. It was unsanitary but delicious.

'Mary Henry', *Carnival of Souls*

After a few months' acquaintance with European 'coffee' one's mind weakens, and his faith with it, and he begins to wonder if the rich beverage of home, with its clotted layer of yellow cream on top of it, is not a mere dream after all, and a thing which never existed.

Mark Twain

A certain Liquor which they call Coffee …
which will soon intoxicate the brain.

G. W. Parry (1601)

Coffee leads men to trifle away their time, scald
their chops, and spend their money, all for a
little base, black, thick, nasty, bitter, stinking
nauseous puddle water.

The Women's Petition Against Coffee (1674)

Moderately drunk, coffee removes vapours from
the brain, occasioned by fumes of wine, or other
strong liquors; eases pains in the head, prevents
sour belchings, and provokes appetite.

England's Happiness Improved (1699)

Coffee, though a useful medicine, if drunk
constantly will at length induce a decay of
health, and hectic fever.

Jesse Torrey, *The Moral Instructor* (1879)

Espresso. It's like coffee-zilla.

'Dean McCoppin', *The Iron Giant*

As soon as coffee is in your stomach, there is a general commotion. Ideas begin to move … similes arise, the paper is covered, coffee is your ally and writing ceases to be a struggle.

Honoré de Balzac

You can tell when you have crossed the frontier into Germany because of the badness of the coffee.

King Edward VII

Well, not much goes on in a one-Starbucks town like Sunnydale.

'Xander', *Buffy the Vampire Slayer*

Coffee has two virtues: it is wet and warm.

Dutch proverb

English coffee tastes like water that has been squeezed out of a wet sleeve.

Fred Allen

Black coffee must be strong and very hot; if strong coffee does not agree with you, do not drink black coffee. And if you do not drink black coffee, do not drink any coffee at all.

André Simon

Coffee makes us severe, and grave, and philosophical.

Jonathan Swift

Coffee is our national misfortune.

Brazilian coffee grower, 1934

Coffee without caffeine is like sex without the spanking.

Trevor 'Cupid' Hale, *Cupid*

Well, I couldn't kill you with Stephen around. I'd have to kill him too, and he's the only one that knows how I like my coffee.

'Robert Green', *The Edge*

I would rather suffer with coffee than be senseless.

Napoleon Bonaparte

The voodoo priest and all his powders were as nothing compared to espresso, cappuccino and mocha, which are stronger than all the religions of the world combined, and perhaps stronger than the human soul itself.

Mark Helprin

You can't smoke in any of these coffee places… I'm pretty sure that coffee was invented by guys who were sitting around smoking anyways, right, and just wanted to drink something that would let them stay up late and smoke f**king more. That's my theory.

Denis Leary

Decaffeinated coffee? Kinda like kissing your sister.

Bob Irwin

100

We would take something old and tired and common – coffee – and weave a sense of romance and community around it. We would rediscover the mystique and charm that had swirled around coffee throughout the centuries.

Howard Schutz, CEO of Starbucks

I'm on a low-fat, high stress diet … coffee and fingernails.

Anon

If you'll excuse me a minute, I'm going to have a cup of coffee.

Broadcast from Apollo 11's LEM, 'Eagle', to Johnson Space Center, Houston, July 20, 1969.

Coffee and cigarettes are much better if you want an instant breakfast.

P. J. O'Rourke

Conscience keeps more people awake than coffee.

Anon

101

Many people claim coffee inspires them, but, as everybody knows, coffee only makes boring people even more boring.

Honoré de Balzac

Strong coffee and plenty, awakens me. It gives me warmth, an unusual force, a pain that is not without pleasure.

Napoleon Bonaparte

He was my cream, and I was his coffee – And when you poured us together, it was something.

Josephine Baker

No one can understand the truth until he drinks of coffee's frothy goodness.

Sheik Abd-al-Kadir

Oh, now this makes me sick. Woman gets four million dollars for spilling coffee on herself. I do that every morning, what do I get? Coffee stains.

'Sergeant Rita Pompano', *Goodbye Lover*

To smoke, and have coffee – and if you do it together, it's fantastic.

Peter Falk, *Der Himmel über Berlin*

Never drink black coffee at lunch; it will keep you awake all afternoon.

Jilly Cooper

I like my coffee like I like my women: in a plastic cup.

Eddie Izzard

You can get every other flavour except coffee-flavoured coffee! They got mochaccino, they got chocaccino, frappaccino, cappaccino, rappaccino, Al Pacino, what the f**k?!

Denis Leary

Coffee is good for talent, but genius wants prayer.

Ralph Waldo Emerson

If I asked for a cup of coffee, someone would search for the double meaning.

Mae West

True, you can sit outside in Paris and drink little cups of coffee, but why this is more stylish than sitting inside and drinking large glasses of whisky I don't know.

P. J. O'Rourke

I don't like fighting fatigue; so I turn to coffee. In town, there's a Starbucks on every corner. In the country, well, no one's invented the corner.

Mike Durrett

Ah, how sweet coffee tastes! Lovelier than a thousand kisses, sweeter far than muscatel wine! I must have coffee.

Johann Sebastian Bach

If you want to improve your understanding, drink coffee; it is the intelligent beverage.

Sydney Smith

Coffee is the common man's gold, and like gold, it brings to every person the feeling of luxury and nobility.

Sheik Abd-al-Kadir

Coffee, according to the women of Denmark, is to the body what the Word of the Lord is to the soul.

Isak Dinesen (Karen Blixen)

Many people are like instant coffee: the minute they get in hot water they dissolve.

Anon

The powers of a man's mind are directly proportional to the quantity of coffee he drinks.

Sir James MacKintosh

If it wasn't for coffee, I'd have no discernible personality at all.

David Letterman

Thank you for your coffee, señor. I shall miss that when we leave Casablanca.

'Ilsa Laszlo', *Casablanca*

The first cup is for the guest, the second for enjoyment, the third for the sword.

Old Arabic proverb

Rock'n'roll is instant coffee.

Bob Geldof

Talkin' about coffee, what's your opinion? Is it a social lubricant or a dangerous stimulant?

'Henry', *Late Bloomers*

The fine line between coffee aficionado and coffee snob is finer than that which divides a perfect espresso from one over-extracted.

Myron Joshua

Instant Human: Just Add Coffee…

Anon

Decaff: Use it to sober up after drinking non-alcoholic beer!

Anon

Drink your coffee! There are poor people in India sleeping!

Anon

True devotees of the café life never restrict themselves to sitting at any single location. Like Don Juans and nymphomaniacs, they are always in search of someplace new.

Daniel Rogov

DRINKING

I spent the whole time battering people I liked and singing with my arm round people I loathed.

Billy Connolly (about his drinking days)

A cocktail party: People who don't like each other particularly, standing around (never enough chairs), talking about things they aren't interested in, drinking drinks they don't want (why set a time to take a drink?) and getting high so that they won't notice they aren't having fun.

Robert Heinlein

Drinking is either an alternative to dating, or the cause of it.

Anon

A good bachelor drinks his dessert (and sometimes the rest of his meals). A sweet tooth is a danger signal that you're getting too much exercise and not enough cocktails.

P. J. O'Rourke

If you drink it straight down, you can feel it going into each individual intestine.

Richard Burton (on raicilla, 180-proof distillate of the maguey plant)

I did quite enjoy the days when one went for a beer at one's local bar in Paris and woke up in Corsica.

Peter O'Toole

Contrary to popular opinion there is not a college education in that bottle; you don't get smarter with every drink you take.

Nathaniel Benchley

Booksellers are good at drinking; librarians are better.

Eliot Fremont-Smith

Journalists today are more into jogging than drinking.

Jay Kovar

Drinking removes warts and wrinkles from women I look at.

Jackie Gleason

If writer's block is soluble in alcohol, so is the liver.

Ernest Lehman

Never accept a drink from a urologist.

Erma Bombeck

Drink up. The world's about to end.

'Ford Prefect', *The Hitchhiker's Guide to the Galaxy*

I shall drink water … it's a mixer Patsy, we have it with whisky.

'Edina', *Absolutely Fabulous*

I used to jog but the ice-cubes kept falling out of my glass.

David Lee Roth

The telephone is a good way to talk to people without having to offer them a drink.

Fran Lebowitz

Beer before liquor – never been sicker, liquor before beer – have no fear.

Anon

I should be dead. I drink very little. Not because I disapprove, not because it's bad for me, simply because I'm not interested in it anymore.

Peter O'Toole

They talk of my drinking but never my thirst.

Scottish proverb

Thirst is the end of drinking and sorrow is the end of drunkenness.

Irish proverb

People may say what they like about the decay of Christianity; the religious system that produced green Chartreuse can never really die.

Saki (H.H. Munro)

A man shouldn't fool with booze until he's 50;
then he's a damn fool if he doesn't.

William Faulkner

Now is the time for drinking, now the time to
beat the earth with unfettered foot.

Horace

I am willing to taste any drink once.

James Cabell

Son, let this be a lesson to you: never do tequila
shooters within a country mile of a marriage
chapel.

'Al Bundy', *Married with Children*

I hadn't the heart to touch my breakfast. I told
Jeeves to drink it himself.

P. G. Wodehouse, *My Man Jeeves*

There are two reasons for drinking; one is, when you are thirsty, to cure it; the other, when you are not thirsty, to prevent it... Prevention is better than cure.

Thomas Love Peacock

Well, then, my stomach must just digest in its waistcoat.

Richard Brinsley Sheridan (after being warned that his drinking would destroy the coat of his stomach)

Drinking provides a beautiful excuse to pursue the one activity that truly gives me pleasure, hooking up with fat hairy girls.

Ross Levy

I decided to stop drinking with creeps. I decided to drink only with friends. I've lost 30 pounds.

Ernest Hemingway

Of all vices, drinking is the most incompatible with greatness.

Sir Walter Scott

A drinker has a hole under his nose that all his money runs into.

Thomas Fuller

Don't drink and drive, you might hit a bump and spill your drink.

Anon

Drink and drive. We need the business.

Bumper sticker on a tow truck

I drink when I have occasion, and sometimes when I have no occasion.

Miguel de Cervantes

Be wary of strong drink. It can make you shoot at tax collectors and miss.

Lazarus Long

Teaching has ruined more American novelists than drink.

Gore Vidal

Where the drink goes in, there the wit goes out.

George Herbert

We are fighting Germany, Austria and drink and as far as I can say the greatest of these three deadly foes is the drink.

David Lloyd George

The first draught serveth for health, the second for pleasure, the third for shame, and the fourth for madness.

Anacharsis

The man that isn't jolly after drinking
Is just a drivelling idiot, to my thinking.

Euripides

Wouldn't it be terrible if I quoted some reliable statistics which prove that more people are driven insane through religious hysteria than by drinking alcohol?

W. C. Fields

115

I don't drink because I have problems or I want to escape. I just love drinking and being drunk.

Richard Harris

When I read about the evils of drinking, I gave up reading.

Henry Youngman

Why does man kill? He kills for food. And not only food: frequently there must be a beverage.

Woody Allen

Electricity is actually made up of extremely tiny particles called electrons, that you cannot see with the naked eye unless you have been drinking.

Dave Barry

LADY ASTOR: Sir, if I were your wife, I'd put poison your drink.
WINSTON CHURCHILL: Madam, if I were your husband, I would drink it.

Reminds me of my safari in Africa. Somebody forgot the corkscrew and for several days we had nothing to live on but food and water.

W. C. Fields

Booze may not be the answer, but it helps you to forget the question.

Lieutenant Henry Mon

There's nothing romantic, nothing grand, nothing heroic, nothing brave, nothing like that about drinking. It's a real coward's death.

Warren Zevon

I drink because she nags, he said
I nag because he drinks.
But if the truth be known to you,
He's a lush and she's a shrew.

Ogden Nash

I drink no more than a sponge.

Francis Rabelais

One drink is too many for me and a thousand not enough.

Brendan Behan

I think I'll have one more before my second last one.

Jack C

Better belly burst than good liquor be lost.

Jonathan Swift

There is this to be said in favour of drinking, that it takes the drunkard first out of society, then out of the world.

Ralph Waldo Emerson

Drunkenness is temporary suicide: the happiness that it brings is merely negative, a momentary cessation of unhappiness.

Bertrand Russell

Man, being reasonable, must get drunk;
The best of life is but intoxication.

> Lord Byron, 'Don Juan'

I often sit back and think, 'I wish I'd done that,'
and find out later that I already have.

> Richard Harris

Drunkenness is nothing but voluntary madness.

> Seneca

A man who exposes himself when he is
intoxicated, has not the art of getting drunk.

> Samuel Johnson

I only drink to make other people seem more
interesting.

> George Jean Nathan

I do not live in the world of sobriety.

> Oliver Reed

It provokes the desire but it takes away the performance. Therefore much drink may be said to be an equivocator with lechery: it makes him and it mars him; it sets him on and it takes him off.

'Porter', *Macbeth*

If merely 'feeling good' could decide, drunkenness would be the supremely valid human experience.

William James

The rapturous, wild, and ineffable pleasure
Of drinking at somebody else's expense.

H. S. Leigh, 'Stanzas to an Intoxicated Fly'

The decline of the aperitif may well be one of the most depressing phenomena of our time.

Luis Buñuel

Drink to me.

Dying words of Pablo Picasso

MacDuff: What three things does drink especially provoke?
Porter: Marry, sir, nose-painting, sleep, and urine.

Macbeth

Under a tattered cloak you will generally find a good drinker.

Spanish proverb

We want the finest wines available to humanity, we want them here, and we want them now!

'Withnail', *Withnail and I*

I always keep a supply of stimulant handy in case I see a snake – which I also keep handy.

W. C. Fields

Up to the age of 40 eating is beneficial. After 40, drinking.

The Talmud, c. 200BC

When a man is forced by circumstance to drink water, you might have the common decency to turn away.

'Private Smalley', *Last Stand at Feather River*

Time is never wasted when you're wasted all the time.

Catherine Zandonella

A drunk man's words are a sober man's thoughts.

Jena Legg

One drink is just right; two are too many; three are too few.

Spanish proverb

No, Sir: There is nothing which has yet been contrived by man by which so much happiness is produced as by a good tavern or inn.

Samuel Johnson, recorded in James Boswell's *Life of Samuel Johnson*, 1776

Drinking when we are not thirsty and making love all year round, madam; that is all there is to distinguish us from other animals.

Pierre-Augustin Caron de Beaumarchais, *The Marriage of Figaro*

I've only been in love with a beer bottle and a mirror.

Sid Vicious

The aim of life is to live, and to live means to be aware, joyously, drunkenly, serenely, divinely aware.

Henry Miller, *Creative Death*

The innkeeper loves a drunkard, but not for a son-in-law.

Jewish proverb

Sherry is dull, naturally dull.

Samuel Johnson

I hate to advocate drugs, alcohol, violence, or insanity to anyone, but they've always worked for me.

Hunter S. Thompson

If penicillin can cure those that are ill, Spanish sherry can bring the dead back to life.

Sir Alexander Fleming

The only time it isn't good for you is when you write or when you fight.

Ernest Hemingway

I drink eternally. For me it is an eternity of drinking, and a drinking up of eternity.

François Rabelais

Now is the time for drinking,
now is the time to make the earth shake with dancing.

Horace

The one conclusive argument that has at all times discouraged people from drinking a poison is not that it kills but rather that it tastes bad.

Friedrich Nietzsche

Drinking spirits cannot cause spiritual damage.

José Bergamín

It is immoral to get drunk because the headache comes after the drinking, but if the headache came first and the drunkenness afterwards, it would be moral to get drunk.

Samuel Butler

A beautiful vacuum filled with wealthy monogamists, all powerful and members of the best families all drinking themselves to death.

Ernest Hemingway, letter to F. Scott Fitzgerald

Alcohol postpones anxiety, then multiplies it.

Mason Cooley

The relationship between a Russian and a bottle of vodka is almost mystical.

Richard Owen

Modern life, too, is often a mechanical oppression and liquor is the only mechanical relief.

Ernest Hemingway

Drinking makes such fools of people, and people are such fools to begin with, that it's compounding a felony.

Robert Benchley

A woman drove me to drink and I never even had the courtesy to thank her.

W. C. Fields

Writing is a lonely job unless you're a drinker, in which case you always have a friend within reach.

Emilio Estevez

I drink too much. I smoke too much. I gamble too much. I AM too much.

'Fitz', *Cracker*

The only way to get a drink out of a Vogon is to stick your fingers down his throat.

'Ford Prefect', *The Hitchhiker's Guide to the Galaxy*

It is better to drink to forget, than to forget to drink.

Anon

Thou shalt not covet thy neighbour's house unless they have a well-stocked bar.

W. C. Fields

Don't forget, you're always fighting. The other fellow is booze. You're evading, always evading, but one of these days, unless you're careful, he's going to nail you.

Irving Berlin to Richard Burton

Alcohol and calculus don't mix... Don't drink and derive.

Anon

You can't drink all day if you don't start in the morning.

Anon

I was tired one night and I went to the bar to have a few drinks. The bartender asked me: 'What'll you have?' I said, 'Surprise me.' He showed me a naked picture of my wife.

Rodney Dangerfield

Some men are like musical glasses; to produce their finest tones you must keep them wet.

Samuel Taylor Coleridge

I don't believe in dining on an empty stomach.

W. C. Fields

Man wants but little drink below, but wants that little strong.

Oliver Wendell Holmes

Back in my rummy days, I would tremble and shake for hours upon arising. It was the only exercise I got.

W. C. Fields

Every man who casts a vote for the saloons deserves that his son shall die a drunkard, or that his daughter should be consigned to the tender mercies of a drunken husband. If you deliberately favour this detestable, crime breeding, filthy blot upon society, you are worse than the saloon keeper. You are so low down that I wouldn't spit on you.

Evangelist, Billy Sunday

I've made it a rule never to drink by daylight and never to refuse a drink after dark.

H. L. Mencken

The worst German enemies we have, who are the greatest menace to the peace and happiness of our people, are Pabst, Schlitz, Miller, Blatz and others of their kind. Their German beer is a far greater enemy to our welfare than German guns or German submarines.

Former Wisconsin Lt. Governor John Strange, 1918

Heaven sent us soda water as a torment for our crimes.

G. K. Chesterton

If you drink like a fish, don't drive. Swim.

Joe E. Louis

Never drink from your finger bowl – it contains only water.

Addison Mizner

Well, we figured now that you're 21, legal drinking age, we should get you a car.

'Billy', *Good Will Hunting*

It has not been the greatest of days – let's put it like that. But my son is basically a good kid really. He will get through this. We are a strong family and we will see him right and we will get to the other side.

Tony Blair (following his 16-year-old son Euan's arrest for being drunk and incapable in Leicester Square)

Anyone who thinks I used to spend my holidays reading political tracts should have come with me for a week. We used to have a pint at every stop – well, the driver's mate did, not the driver, thankfully – and we used to have about 10 stops in a day.

William Hague (interview in *GQ* magazine)

It's not what isn't, it's what you wish WAS that makes unhappiness ... I think too much. That's why I drink.

Janis Joplin

I'm Catholic and I can't commit suicide, but I plan to drink myself to death.

Jack Kerouac

I tried to imagine my future, ten years from now, and I don't want to be some drunken geezer who's stumbling around.

Noel Gallagher

I don't know if my wife left me because of my drinking or I started drinking 'cause my wife left me.

'Ben Sanderson', *Leaving Las Vegas*

Drinking doesn't cause hangovers, waking up does!

Anon

I am not drunk! I am by nature a loud, friendly, clumsy person.

Anon

I've used up all my sick days so now I'm calling in drunk.

Anon

How can I be so thirsty this morning when I drank so much last night?

Anon

That's nice talk, Ben – keep drinking. Between the 101-proof breath and the occasional bits of drool, some interesting words come out.

'Sera', *Leaving Las Vegas*

Eat, drink and be merry, for tomorrow they may make it illegal.

Anon

My grandmother is over 80 and still doesn't need glasses. Drinks right out of the bottle.

Henny Youngman

The church is near, but the road is icy. The tavern is far, but we will walk carefully.

Russian proverb

Bibo, ergo sum (I drink, therefore I am.)

Anon

I don't care how liberated this world becomes –
a man will always be judged by the amount of
alcohol he can consume – and a woman will be
impressed, whether she likes it or not.

'Doug', *Cocktail*

Drink not the third glass, which thou canst not
tame when once it is within thee.

George Herbert

Much has been written and said about the most
successful ways to open and carry on a conversation but none surpasses 'What are you
drinking?'

Bill Bowyang's Magazine (July 1927)

Wasting time is an important part of living.

Anon

A red nose never lost a friend worth holding.

Evelyn Waugh

But men do not drink for the effect alcohol produces on the body. What they drink for is the brain-effect; and if it must come through the body, so much worse for the body.

Jack London, *John Barleycorn*

Drink, in reality, doth not reverse nature, or create passions in men which did not exist in them before.

Henry Fielding, *Tom Jones*

He was always ashamed when he had to drive after he had been drinking, always apologetic to the horse.

D. H. Lawrence, *The Rainbow*

Booze and religion have very similar effects. They both make you stupid and they both make you see things that aren't there.

Anon

Anything worth doing is worth overdoing.

Anon

Who needs friends when you can sit alone in your room and drink?

Anon

DRUGS

The government could take away all the drugs in the world and people would spin around on their lawns until they fell down and saw God.

Dennis Miller

As long as there's, you know, sex and drugs, I can do without the rock and roll.

'Mick Shrimpton', *This Is Spinal Tap*

Most people don't know how they're gonna feel from one moment to the next. But a dope fiend has a pretty good idea. All you gotta do is look at the labels on the little bottles.

'Bob', *Drugstore Cowboy*

Any country that can survive Stalin can certainly handle a little dope.

Viktor Rostavili, *Red Heat*

Rule number one: don't underestimate the other guy's greed. Rule number two: don't get high on your own supply.

'Frank', *Scarface*

It was good to be alive. But the intellectual part of myself asked 'What is different to normal? Why isn't life always like this?' I deduced that I was simply allowing myself to enjoy what had always been there. I realised that I had got into the habit of restraining myself.

Nicholas Saunders, *E for Ecstasy*

137

Alexander Shulgin told the story of a Japanese poet who tried MDMA and said: 'It has taken 20 years of studying Zen for me to reach this clarity, but I'm glad I did it my way.'

Nicholas Saunders, *E for Ecstasy*

Absinthe makes the heart grow fonder.

Addison Mizner

The other day they asked me about mandatory drug testing. I said I believed in drug testing a long time ago. All through the '60s I tested everything.

Bill Lee

Police have arrested the man who was pictured throwing snowballs at Giants Stadium. If convicted, he may face six months in jail and a $1,000 fine. If it turns out he was under the influence of alcohol or drugs, he'll be signed by the Yankees.

David Letterman

They were both high. They'd been smokin' everything but their shoes.

'Clairee Belcher', *Steel Magnolias*

Using drugs isn't cheating. It's stealing victory from someone who deserves it.

Ian Thorpe, swimmer

A miracle drug is any drug that will do what the label says it will do.

Eric Hodgins

The last time somebody said, 'I find I can write much better with a word processor,' I replied, 'They used to say the same thing about drugs.'

Roy Blount, Jr

I would advise you to keep your head down, avoid a major drug habit, play every day, and take it in front of other people.

James Taylor

You can turn your back on a person, but never turn your back on a drug. Especially when it's waving a razor-sharp hunting knife in your eye.

'Raoul Duke', *Fear and Loathing in Las Vegas*

I do not take drugs. I am drugs.

Salvador Dali

There's no point in saying, 'I don't have an idea today, so I'll just smoke some drugs.' You should stay alert for the moment when a number of things are just ready to collide with one another.

Brian Eno

It is better to burn out than fade away.

Kurt Cobain

Everything is a dangerous drug to me except reality, which is unendurable.

Cyril Connolly

I used to have a drug problem, now I make enough money.

David Lee Roth

I never had a problem with drugs, only with cops.

Keith Richards

I heard that your brain stops growing when you start doing drugs. Let's see, I guess that makes me 19.

Steven Tyler, Aerosmith

I'm glad they didn't have drugs [in] the '60s when I was in high school, because if they'd had drugs I'd still be in high school.

Joe Walsh, The Eagles

I am sure we were meant to take drugs because otherwise we wouldn't get stoned.

Howard Marks

I mean the fact there are all these receptors in the brain all ready to react to these things coming in would suggest some kind of semiotic relationship between animals and drugs that's being going on for several million years.

Howard Marks

Guns are always the best method for private suicide. Drugs are too chancy. You might just miscalculate the dosage and just have a good time.

P. J. O'Rourke

I don't need drugs. Life is already tragic enough.

Eddie Vedder

Drugs? Everyone has a choice and I choose not to do drugs.

Leonardo DiCaprio

Avoid all needle drugs – the only dope worth shooting is Richard Nixon.

Abbie Hoffman

Drug therapies are replacing a lot of medicines as we used to know it.

George W. Bush

Drug misuse is not a disease, it is a decision, like the decision to step out in front of a moving car. You would not call that a disease but an error of judgement.

Philip K. Dick

Maybe a nation that consumes as much booze and dope as we do and has our kind of divorce statistics should pipe down about 'character issues'.

P. J. O'Rourke

I said 'no' to drugs, but they just wouldn't listen.

Bumper sticker

I don't like people who take drugs: customs men for example.

Mick Miller

I may kid around about drugs, but really, I take them seriously.

Doctor Graper

Drugs are a bet with your mind.

Jim Morrison

If you are going to get wasted, then get wasted elegantly.

Keith Richards

People say I get on a power trip when I snort blow. I respond simply by saying I'm bigger and better than you.

Anon

If people take any notice of what we say, we say we've been through the drug scene, man, and there's nothing like being straight.

John Lennon

The Beatles were so high they even let Ringo sing a couple of songs.

Bill Hicks

Don't drink and drive, get high and fly home!

Anon

Take me, I am the drug; take me, I am hallucinogenic.

Salvador Dali

The worst drugs are as bad as anybody's told you... It's just a dumb trip, which I can't condemn people if they get into it, because one gets into it for one's own personal, social, emotional reasons. It's something to be avoided if one can help it.

John Lennon

OPIATE, *n.* An unlocked door in the prison of Identity. It leads into the jail yard.

Ambrose Bierce, *The Devil's Dictionary*

The human mind is capable of excitement without the application of gross and violent stimulants; and he must have a very faint perception of its beauty and dignity who does not know this.

William Wordsworth

It's an ordinary day for Brian. Like, he died every day, you know.

Pete Townshend (on Brian Jones's death by drowning in July 1969).

If you think dope is for kicks and for thrills, you're out of your mind. There are more kicks to be had in a good case of paralytic polio or by living in an iron lung. If you think you need stuff to play music or sing, you're crazy. It can fix you so you can't play nothing or sing nothing.

Billie Holiday

Words are, of course, the most powerful drug used by mankind.

Rudyard Kipling

Poetry is a mere drug, Sir.

George Farquhar

Drugs are a one-man birthday party.

P. J. O'Rourke

Drugs are marvellous – it's life that's evil. And sometimes the only way to face it is to get completely twisted.

E. Jean Carroll

Success and failure are both difficult to endure. Along with success come drugs, divorce, fornication, bullying, travel, meditation, medication, depression, neurosis and suicide. With failure comes failure.

Joseph Heller

If you can remember anything about the '60s, you weren't really there.

Paul Kantner

Half of the modern drugs could well be thrown out of the window, except that the birds might eat them.

Martin H. Fischer

I never took hallucinogenic drugs because I never wanted my consciousness expanded one unnecessary iota.

Fran Lebowitz

Chicken Soup: An ancient miracle drug containing equal parts of aureomycin, cocaine, interferon, and TLC. The only ailment chicken soup can't cure is neurotic dependence on one's mother.

Arthur Naiman

I awoke from The Sickness at the age of 45, calm and sane, and in reasonably good health except for a weakened liver and the look of borrowed flesh common to all who survive The Sickness...

William Burroughs

Drugs bring us to the gates of paradise, then keep us from entering.

Mason Cooley

I'm a junkie. I like drugs, I like the whole lifestyle, but it just didn't pay off.

'Bob', *Drugstore Cowboy*

Reality is just a crutch for people who can't cope with drugs.

Robin Williams

In Manchester, you either become a musician, a footballer, a drugs dealer or work in a factory. And there aren't a lot of factories left, y'know.

Noel Gallagher

Run for office? No, I have slept with too many women, done too many drugs and been to too many parties.

George Clooney

A drug is that substance which, when injected into a rat, will produce a scientific report.

Anonymous

I spent most of my money on booze, drugs and women… The rest I wasted.

W. C. Fields

Drugs may be the road to nowhere, but at least they're the scenic route!

Anon

Just Say No to Drugs.

Nancy Reagan

Every generation finds the drug it needs.

P. J. O'Rourke

Parents! Studies have shown that taking your kids to the library reduces the likelihood that they will try drugs.

NY subway poster campaign slogan

My all-time favourite drug slogan comes from a television ad. It features a young, fiercely 'independent' teen, who looks defiantly into the camera and proclaims, 'I don't need to do drugs to be cool'. Well hell, you could say that about anything society 'tells us' we need to do in order to fit in, e.g., 'I don't need to take baths to be cool'.

Bob Murphy

I don't do illegal drugs anymore. Now I just do the legal drugs. Tonight I'm on NyQuil and Sudafed.

Denis Leary

Drugs are marvellous if you want to escape, but reality is so rich, why escape?

Geraldine Chaplin

The only way to get rid of a temptation is to yield to it.

Oscar Wilde

The best mind-altering drug is truth.

Lily Tomlin

To really enjoy drugs you've got to want to get out of where you are. But there are some wheres that are harder to get out of than others. This is the drug-taking problem for adults. Teenage weltschmerz is easy to escape. But what drug will get a grown-up out of, for instance, debt?

P. J. O'Rourke

Critics have told me I've ruined the lives of 50 million young people. I can't be certain of this, since only about 10 million have ever come back to thank me.

Timothy Leary

Most [trippers] would rather change their way of looking at reality, than face the difficult and discouraging task of transforming reality itself.

David Arora

What gets lost in abbreviation – Prozac cures! Heroin kills! – is that drugs work because the human body works, and they fail or hurt us because the body and spirit are vulnerable.

Joshua Wolf Shenk

I remember when I swallowed a bottle of sleeping pills. My doctor told me to have a few drinks and get some rest.

Rodney Dangerfield

We have reached the point where the over-the-counter drugs are actually stronger than anything you can buy on the street.

Denis Leary

The young physician starts life with 20 drugs for each disease, and the old physician ends life with one drug for 20 diseases.

William Osler

I need a valium the size of a hockey puck.

'Danny Rose', *Broadway Danny Rose*

I've used speed briefly, like for a day for writing, but the use of speed over two days tends to lead to irritability and insistency and a kind of Hitlerian fascist mentality, which may be the byproducts of real perceptions of interest.

Allen Ginsberg

Tobacco, coffee, alcohol, hashish, prussic acid, strychnine are weak dilutions: the surest poison is time.

Ralph Waldo Emerson

I'm not interested in being Wonder Woman in the delivery room. Give me drugs.

Madonna (requesting an epidural in 1996)

Love is the drug which makes sexuality palatable in popular mythology.

Germaine Greer

A gramme is better than a damn.

Aldous Huxley, *Brave New World*

The world is having a nervous breakdown.
Valium is the only glue that holds it together.

Arthur Janov

Oh, jab me with your needle a hundred times
And a hundred times I will bless you, Saint
Morphine.

Jules Verne

Take a holiday from reality whenever you like,
and come back without so much as a headache
or a mythology.

Aldous Huxley, *Brave New World*

By the mid '60s I had become such a dope fiend
that I kept my entire stash in a bank-vault
deposit box.

Paul Krassner

A rose is a rose is a rose. But these chair legs
were chair legs were St. Michael and all angels.

Aldous Huxley (describing the effects of mescalin)

I never turned blue in somebody else's bathroom. I consider that the height of bad manners.

Keith Richards

In his ordinary consciousness man lives like someone trying to speak in an excessively sensitive echo-chamber; he can proceed only by doggedly ignoring the interminably gibbering reflections of his voice.

Alan W. Watts

Speed was originally invented by the Germans for use by the pilots in bombing England, so it's originally a kind of totalitarian synthetic.

Allen Ginsberg

I'm proving that if you're on drugs then you're in trouble because those drugs aren't working. I'm clean and I'm beating you.

Linford Christie

The ideal government agency to deal with speed freaks would be a whole bunch of lumberjacks up in the mountains and strong peasant girls to cook flap-jacks and make a fire; and let the speed demon sleep off his depression and lie around for a couple of weeks until he finally feels like going out and smelling the evergreens and then maybe building a fence or a bridge back.

Allen Ginsberg

The only recurring dreams I can remember are all on cold turkey, and it was always that the dope was hidden behind the wallpaper. And in the morning, you'd wake up and see fingernail marks where you actually tried to do something about it.

Keith Richards

You are never the same after you've had that one flash glimpse down the cellular time tunnel. You are never the same after you've had the veil drawn.

Timothy Leary

My life then basically was 'Do I have the dope to start this day off? Can I make it until the next fix?' You think you're in this elite club. You could be wallowing in the gutter and think, 'I'm elite.' It was an adventurous experiment that went on too long.

Keith Richards

Once we recognise the importance and value of other states of consciousness, we can begin to teach people, particularly the young, how to satisfy their needs without drugs.

Andrew Weil

Drugs snatch us out of everyday reality, blur our perception, alter our sensations, and, in a word, put the entire universe in a state of suspension.

Octavio Paz

Don't do drugs because if you do drugs you'll go to prison, and drugs are really expensive in prison.

John Hardwick

I'd always done a lot of glue as a kid. I was very interested in glue, and then I went to lager and speed, and I drifted into heroin because as a kid growing up everybody told me, 'Don't smoke marijuana, it will kill you.'

Irvine Welsh

How we ever actually managed to do any burgling, I don't know. We were all off our tits on drugs.

Noel Gallagher

I chose to do drugs. I don't feel sorry for myself at all, but have nothing good to say about them. They are a total waste of time.

Kurt Cobain

The kid couldn't cope.

Keith Richards on the death of Kurt Cobain

Drugs. I can take them or leave them. But they're much more effective when I take them.

Ronnie Shakes

Every culture throughout history has made use of chemicals to alter consciousness except the Eskimos, who had to wait for the white man to bring them alcohol, since they could not grow anything.

Andrew Weil

I didn't need drugs to have experiences, I had always had experiences without drugs, and so anything like that would impair them. Alcohol would impair them. It produces a false ecstasy.

Van Morrison

I would say that 99 per cent of people misuse, abuse drugs right now. But that's not the problem of the brain, the brain is perfect, nor the drugs because the drugs are pretty good – if you know how to use them. It's simply a fault of poor education.

Timothy Leary

I've abused drugs, but I didn't go into them without boning up first.

Keith Richards

What is dangerous about the tranquilliser is that whatever peace of mind they bring is a packaged peace of mind. Where you buy a pill and buy peace with it, you get conditioned to cheap solutions instead of deep ones.

Max Lerner

A man who cannot work without his hypodermic needle is a poor doctor. The amount of narcotic you use is inversely proportional to your skill.

Martin H. Fischer

I will lift up mine eyes unto the pills. Almost everyone takes them, from the humble aspirin to the multi-coloured, king-sized three deckers, which put you to sleep, wake you up, stimulate and soothe you all in one. It is an age of pills.

Malcolm Muggeridge

There is nothing wrong with you that some Prozac and a polo mallet wouldn't fix.

Woody Allen, *New York Murder Mystery*

If you want idiot happiness take tranquillisers, or pray for senility. Anxiety is inevitable and periodic depression is normal.

Leo Rosten

There's only one fatal disease, I've concluded. It's called hypochondria. And it is deadly.

Keith Richards

I believe in a long, prolonged, derangement of the senses in order to obtain the unknown.

Jim Morrison

There's high, and there's high, and to get really high – I mean so high that you can walk on the water, that high – that's where I'm going.

George Harrison

I hope the fans will take up meditation instead of drugs.

Ringo Starr

I now realise that taking drugs was like taking an aspirin without having a headache.

Paul McCartney

It has always been interesting to me that the concept of drug treatment programs usually had a lot to do with what drug could be used to help someone get off of drugs.

Dr. Marc D'Andrea

I only ever get ill when I give up drugs.

Keith Richards

It is all right letting yourself go, as long as you can get yourself back.

Mick Jagger

I don't want my daughter to grow up and some-day be hassled by kids at school … I don't want people telling her that her parents were junkies.

Kurt Cobain

I knew that when I had a child, I'd be over-whelmed and it's true . . . I can't tell you how much my attitude has changed since we've got Frances. Holding my baby is the best drug in the world.

Kurt Cobain

Let's just say I was testing the bounds of reality. I was curious to see what would happen. That's all it was: just curiosity.

Jim Morrison

All I need is one final hit to soothe the pain while the Valium takes effect.

'Mark "Rent-boy" Renton', *Trainspotting*

If I die, tell Rolling Stone that my last words were 'I'm on drugs!'

'Russell Hammond', *Almost Famous*

The road of excess leads to the palace of wisdom.

William Blake

Jimi Hendrix deceased, drugs. Janis Joplin deceased, alcohol. Mama Cass deceased, ham sandwich.

'Austin Powers', *Austin Powers: International Man of Mystery*

See, the Bible says 'big fish' and everybody assumes, 'a whale'. Whereas I think: 'drugs'.

Jeremy 'Moondog' Young

The most beautiful experience we can have is the mysterious; it is the fundamental emotion which stands at the cradle of true art and true science.

Albert Einstein

Ecstasy, at least it's not crack.

Anon

Only users lose drugs.

Anon

Every now and then when your life gets complicated and the weasels start closing in, the only
real cure is to load up on heinous chemicals and
then drive like a bastard from Hollywood to Las
Vegas.

Hunter S. Thompson

There are only two industries on this planet that
would use such a sneering term like 'user' for its
customers: the computer industry and the drug
cartels. They both have an equal lack of respect
for the poor, miserable souls who have to use
their crummy products.

Paul Saffo

Your mind is like a parachute; it works better
when it's HIGH!

Anon

I had to quit smoking crack. The last time I
smoked so much I robbed my own house.

Anon

It may not be a tragedy. I don't think it's a normal part of growing up.

'Drugs czar', Keith Hellawell (contemplating a young person, such as one of his grandchildren, trying drugs)

New York police department ... has been unable to make a narcotics case on the Lennons.

FBI secret files

There is always a need for intoxication: China has opium, Islam has hashish, the West has women.

André Malraux

There was an encounter with what can only be described as an elf hive, a colony of self-transforming, hyperdimensional machine creatures that came bounding forward with joyful squeaks to dribble themselves like self-transforming jeweled basketballs on the floor in front of me, and I was dumbstruck with amazement.

Terence McKenna describing a DMT trip

Some people drink, and some don't; some
people like to smoke a bowl, and some don't.
Some people do and some people don't but it's
OK 'cause it was meant to be that way.

Dave Mathews

For art to exist, for any sort of aesthetic activity
or perception to exist, a certain physiological
precondition is indispensable: intoxication.

Friedrich Nietzsche

It is possible that a certain amount of brain
damage is of therapeutic value.

Dr. Paul Hoch

Marxism is the opiate of the unstoned classes.

Arthur Kleps

The drug user drowns in the same pool mystics
swim in.

Joseph Campbell

Occasionally people ask me 'Is DMT
[dimethyltryptamine] dangerous?', and I think
the honest answer is 'only if you fear death by
astonishment'.

Terence McKenna

Man's first civilisations gave great place to
intoxication. Long before there was decadence
or world weariness, men and women wanted to
change their response to the planet on which
they had evolved to self consciousness.

Jacquetta Hawkes

Chemistry is applied theology.

Augustus Owsley Stanley

Drugs don't take people, people take drugs.

Abbie Hoffman

Drugs are the product of Satan. Drug users need
to be saved by the Holy Power of Jesus Christ.

William John Bennett

Drugs have taught an entire generation of
American kids the metric system.

P. J. O'Rourke

Only drugs make you feel as good as the people
in TV ads appear to be.

Hakim Bey

When the conscious becomes unconscious,
you're drunk. When the unconscious becomes
conscious, you're stoned.

Anon

Not that which goeth into the mouth defileth a
man: but that which cometh out of the mouth,
this defileth a man.

Matthew 15:11

I'm tired of being number one on the naughty
boys drug poll. It's time they picked on someone
else.

Keith Richards

Stay away from drugs, gangs and cyberporn on the Internet and you can be President some day.

'Elwood Blues', *Blues Brothers 2000*

Drugs ain't a black thing, or a white thing. It's a death thing. Death don't give a shit about colour.

'Nick Peretti', *New Jack City*

I haven't been this happy since it was OK to take drugs.

'Lilly', *That Old Feeling*

Why do they call it experimenting with drugs? It's just experimenting with ill health.

Paul Morrissey

Marx said religion was the opiate of the people, but I'm afraid today it's more like a runaway meth lab.

Susie Bright

DRUGS WAR

Evidence proves that prohibition only drives drunkenness behind doors and into dark places, and does not cure it or even diminish it.

Mark Twain

Prohibition? HA! They tried that in the movies and it didn't work.

Homer Simpson

In our culture we think we're not having a good time unless we're legless. If I could legalise one, tobacco, alcohol or soft drugs, it would be cannabis.

Dr Mark Porter

I am 100 per cent in favour of the intelligent use of drugs and 1000 per cent against the thoughtless use of them, whether caffeine or LSD.

Timothy Leary

Today and every day this year, 3,000 young people will begin to smoke; 1,000 of them ultimately will die of cancer, emphysema, heart disease and other diseases caused by smoking. That's more than a million vulnerable young people a year being hooked on nicotine that ultimately could kill them.

Bill Clinton

Prohibition is better than no liquor at all.

Will Rogers

Acute deaths related solely to cocaine, amphetamines or ecstasy are unusual, despite the publicity they receive.

European Monitoring Centre for Drugs and Drug Addiction report

I just cannot, you know, believe in a war against drugs when they've got anti-drug commercials on TV all day long, followed by, 'This Bud's for you'.

Bill Hicks

One thing about drugs, they certainly cause psychosis in bureaucrats who haven't taken them.

Timothy Leary

Instead of all of this energy and effort directed at the war to end drugs, how about a little attention to drugs which will end war?

Albert Hofmann

Prohibition makes you want to cry into your beer and denies you the beer to cry into.

Don Marquis

If people are good only because they fear punishment, and hope for reward, then we are a sorry lot indeed.

Albert Einstein

We need a World War II-style victory campaign for a drug-free America.

Newt Gingrich

We won't dispassionately investigate or rationally debate which drugs do what damage and whether or how much of that damage is the result of criminalisation. We'd rather work ourselves into a screaming fit of puritanism and then go home and take a pill.

P. J. O'Rourke

Only one out of every thousand LSD users reported a negative experience, yet the press dug up a thousand lucid stories of bark-eating Princeton grads.

Timothy Leary

Let us declare nature to be legitimate. All plants should be declared legal, and all animals for that matter. The notion of illegal plants and animals is obnoxious and ridiculous.

Terence McKenna

We're not really going to get anywhere until we take the criminality out of drugs.

Former Secretary of State, George P. Schultz

I think it can be truthfully said that any man who wants a drink can get one, and about the only difference between the present condition, and the condition preceding Prohibition is that the man who wants to take a mild drink is compelled to take a strong one, and a man who wants a good drink is compelled to take a bad one.

William Randolph Hearst

Alcohol didn't cause the high crime rates of the '20s and '30s, Prohibition did. And drugs do not cause today's alarming crime rates, but drug prohibition does.

US District Judge, James C. Paine

Ann Widdecombe announced zero tolerance of drugs again yesterday – but … unfortunately displayed almost zero common sense.

Daily Telegraph

I associate my experience with drugs (soft ones) not with Mick Jagger or Aldous Huxley but with passing my law degree and working in a bank.

Tory MP, David Prior, 1998

There is no moral middle ground. Indifference is not an option… For the sake of our children, I implore each of you to be unyielding and inflexible in your opposition to drugs.

Nancy Reagan

Of course drugs were fun. And that's what's so stupid about anti-drug campaigns: they don't admit that.

Anjelica Huston

If the words 'life, liberty, and the pursuit of happiness' don't include the right to experiment with your own consciousness, then the Declaration of Independence isn't worth the hemp it was written on.

Terence McKenna

People hate themselves anyway. If it wasn't smack, they'd hate themselves for eating carrots. You can bet on it.

Keith Richards

In Al Gore's $500 million crime plan, he has called for drug testing of prison inmates. What happens if you flunk the test, do you go to prison prison? You are already in prison.

Jay Leno

Nobody's got the right to judge over what I am putting into my body, apart from myself.

Keith Richards

Education, guns, drugs, school prayer, gays, defence spending, taxes – you name it, we disagree.

'President Bartlet', *The West Wing*

Could I speak to the drug dealer of the house, please?

'Jack Slater', *Last Action Hero*

Casual drug users ought to be taken out and shot.

Daryl Gates, Los Angeles police chief

In economics there's a law called Gresham's Law that bad money drives out good money – paper money will drive out gold. The very opposite is true in the sociology of drugs. Good drugs drive out bad drugs.

Timothy Leary

I don't know about you, but I rather enjoy the way tax money is spent to arrest, indict, convict, imprison, parole and then re-imprison these people [drug users]. I'd just piss it away on beer, anyway.

Lenny Bruce

The most insidious influence on the young is not violence, drugs, tobacco, drink or sexual perversion, but our pursuit of the trivial and our tolerance of the third-rate.

Eric Anderson (former headmaster of Eton)

A drug is not bad. A drug is a chemical compound. The problem comes in when people who take drugs treat them like a licence to behave like an asshole.

Frank Zappa

All drugs of any interest to any moderately intelligent person in America are now illegal.

Thomas Szasz

There is held to be no surer test of civilisation than the increase per head of the consumption of alcohol and tobacco. Yet alcohol and tobacco are recognisable poisons, so that their consumption has only to be carried far enough to destroy civilisation altogether.

Havelock Ellis

Let us not forget who we are. Drug abuse is a repudiation of everything America is.

Ronald Reagan

My thinking tends to be libertarian. That is, I oppose intrusions of the state into the private realm – as in abortion, sodomy, prostitution, pornography, drug use, or suicide, all of which I would strongly defend as matters of free choice in a representative democracy.

Camille Paglia

To punish drug takers is like a drunk striking the bleary face it sees in the mirror.

Brian Inglis

Only one thing is certain: if pot is legalised, it won't be for our benefit but for the authorities'. To have it legalised will also be to lose control of it.

Germaine Greer

If we can get them to understand that saying 'no' to drugs is rebelling against their parents and the generations of the past, we'd make it an enormous success.

John Van de Kamp

Working together we can treat Washington's 40 billion dollar a year addiction to the War on Drugs.

Polly Wilmoth, Waco, Texas

There seems to be no stopping drug frenzy once it takes hold of a nation. What starts with an innocuous HUGS, NOT DRUGS bumper sticker soon leads to wild talk of shooting dealers and making urine tests a condition for employment – anywhere.

Barbara Ehrenreich

Drug dealers and politicians have always been aligned on the same side of the drug prohibition issue: To politicians, the support of drug prohibition means votes; to the drug purveyors, it means money.

James E. Gierach

Our generation is the first ever to have made the search for self-awareness a crime.

Alexander Shulgin

At a time when we are pleading with foreign governments to stop the export of cocaine, it is the height of hypocrisy for the United States to export tobacco.

Everett C. Koop

The prestige of the government has undoubtedly been lowered considerably by the Prohibition Law. Nothing is more destructive of respect for the government and the law of the land than passing laws which cannot be enforced.

Albert Einstein

If you say 'Would there were no wine,' because of the drunkards, then you must say, going on by degrees, 'Would there were no steel,' because of the murderers, 'Would there were no night,' because of the thieves, 'Would there were no light,' because of the informers, and 'Would there were no women,' because of adultery.

Saint John Chrysostom (c. AD345)

Instead of giving money to found colleges to promote learning, why don't they pass a consti-tutional amendment prohibiting anybody from learning anything? If it works as good as the Prohibition one did, why, in five years we would have the smartest race of people on earth.

Will Rogers

American prohibitionism ... has done more than anything else to corrupt the police and foster disrespect for law, and which our economic pressure has, in the special problem of drug abuse, spread to the rest of the world.

Alan Watts

Understand that legal and illegal are political, and often arbitrary, categorisations; use and abuse are medical, or clinical, distinctions.

Abbie Hoffman

Although man is already 90 per cent water, the Prohibitionists are not yet satisfied.

John Kendrick Bangs

The 'just say no' campaign at this point is a lot like drawing sea-monsters over certain unexplored areas of the map and expecting people to stay away. It may work for some, but explorers live for this kind of thing.

Terence McKenna

What are politicians going to tell people when the Constitution is gone and we still have a drug problem?

William Simpson

I'm a prohibitionist. What I propose to prohibit is the reckless use of water.

Bob Edwards

Authorities are now saying that the war on drugs will be bigger than World War II... Oh, great ... more Time-Life books.

Jay Leno

For every prohibition you create you also create an underground.

Jello Biafra

Just Say No did something insidious. It reduced the debate to a single word.

Dan Baum

In Britain there is a death from heroin approximately once a week, from alcohol once an hour, and from tobacco every five minutes.

www.drugtext.org

DRUNKENNESS

O that men should put an enemy in their mouths to steal away their brains.

William Shakespeare, *Othello*

The best audience is intelligent, well-educated,
and a little drunk.

Alben William Barkley

My dad was the town drunk. Usually that's not
so bad, but New York City?

Henny Youngman

Most Americans are born drunk, and really
require a little wine or beer to sober them. They
have a sort of permanent intoxication from
within, a sort of invisible champagne.

G. K. Chesterton

Hamlet is a coarse and barbarous play. One
might think the work is the product of a
drunken savage's imagination.

Voltaire

Drink, and be mad, then; 'tis your country bids!
Gloriously drunk, obey th'important call!

William Cowper

I've never been happier than I was as a drunk.

Frank Skinner

I drink until I'm drunk. Then I go on drinking until I think I'm sober. Then I know I'm drunk.

Anon

Is there anything more beautiful than a beautiful, beautiful flamingo flying across in front of a beautiful sunset. And he has a beautiful rose in his beak. And also he is carrying a very beautiful painting in his feet. And also, you're drunk.

Jack Handy

Anybody can be a non-drunk. It takes a special talent to be a drunk. It takes endurance. Endurance is more important than truth.

'Henry', *Barfly*

I am as drunk as a lord, but then, I am one, so what does it matter?

Bertrand Russell

A man, indeed, is not genteel when he gets drunk; but most vices may be committed very genteelly: a man may debauch his friend's wife genteelly; he may cheat at cards genteelly.

James Boswell

Cambridge has seen many strange sights. It has seen Wordsworth drunk, it has seen Porson sober. I am a greater scholar than Wordsworth and I am a greater poet than Porson. So I fall betwixt and between.

A. E. Housman

Grant stood by me when I was crazy and I stood by him when he was drunk.

William Sherman (US general and president)

What, when drunk, one sees in other women, one sees in Garbo sober.

Kenneth Tynan

Karl Marx wasn't a Marxist all the time. He got drunk in the Tottenham Court Road.

Michael Foot

There are, it is true, still a few minor points of life which may serve to demarcate the upper class, but they are only minor ones . . . when drunk, gentlemen often become amorous or maudlin or vomit in public, but they never become truculent.

Alan Ross

I know better than to get tight oftener than once in three months. It sets a man back in the esteem of people whose opinions are worth having.

Mark Twain

Life is a waste of time, time is a waste of life, so get wasted all of the time and have the time of your life.

Michelle Mastrolacasa

Of the demonstrably wise there are but two:
those who commit suicide and those who keep
their reasoning faculties atrophied with drink.

Mark Twain

People who drink to drown their sorrow should
be told that sorrow knows how to swim.

Ann Landers

Any man that had any respect for himself would
have got drunk, as was the custom of the
country on all occasions of public moment.

Mark Twain

A drunkard is like a whisky-bottle, all neck and
belly and no head.

Anon

I was daily intoxicated, yet no man could call
me intemperate.

Henry David Thoreau

Never refuse to do a kindness unless the act would work great injury to yourself, and never refuse to take a drink – under any circumstances.

Mark Twain

One tequila, two tequila, three tequila, floor.

Anon

Drunkenness is the rain of reason. It is premature old age. It is temporary death.

Saint Basil

Three highballs and I think I'm St Francis of Assisi.

Dorothy Parker

My advice to you is to start drinking heavily.

'Bluto', *Animal House*

The secret of drunkenness is, that it insulates us in thought, whilst it unites us in feeling.

Ralph Waldo Emerson

C'mon, Moe. It's been St. Patrick's day for hours now and I'm not drunk yet!

Homer Simpson

Drunkenness is not a mere matter of intoxicating liquors; it goes deeper, far deeper. Drunkenness is the failure of a man to control his thoughts.

David Grayson

I love a drink, but I never encouraged drunkenness by harping on its alleged funny side.

Mark Twain

I'm not under the alkafluence of inkahol that some thinkle peep I am.

Anon

The drunker I sit here the longer I get.

Anon

Drunkenness is the vice of a good constitution,
or of a bad memory.

Colton

A drunk man's tongue is a sober man's mind.

Anon

No animal ever invented anything so bad as
drunkenness – or so good as drink.

G. K. Chesterton

Drunk is feeling sophisticated when you can't
say it.

Anon

The problem with some people is that when
they aren't drunk they're sober.

William Butler Yeats

The hard part about being a bartender is figuring out who is drunk and who is just stupid.

Richard Braunstein

A meal without wine is like a day without sunshine, except that on a day without sunshine you can still get drunk.

Lee Entrekin

University – where the average drunk goes to get drunker than average!

Anon

I stopped drinking 'cause I had a problem. I'd get pulled over by the cops and start dancing to their lights thinking I'd made it to another club!

Bill Hicks

Other countries drink to get drunk, and this is accepted by everyone; in France, drunkenness is a consequence, never an intention. A drink is felt as the spinning out of a pleasure, not as the

necessary cause of an effect which is sought:
wine is not only a philtre, it is also the leisurely
act of drinking.

Roland Barthes

When I played drunks I had to remain sober
because I didn't know how to play them when I
was drunk.

Richard Burton

I prefer to think that God is not dead, just
drunk.

John Huston

Don't you know there ain't no devil, it's just God
when he's drunk.

Tom Waits

Drunkenness does not create vice; it merely
brings it into view.

Seneca

Actually it only takes me one drink to get drunk. The trouble is I can't remember if it's the 13th or 14th.

George Burns

I have never been drunk, but often I've been overserved.

George Gobel

No nation was ever drunk when wine was cheap.

Thomas Jefferson

All excess is ill, but drunkenness is of the worst sort. It spoils health, dismounts the mind, and unmans men. It reveals secrets, is quarrelsome, lascivious, impudent, dangerous and bad.

William Penn

Since the creation of the world there has been no tyrant like intemperance and no slaves so cruelly treated as his.

William Garrison

When a man has been intemperate so long that shame no longer paints a blush upon his cheek, his liquor generally does it instead.

George Prentice

Indulgences, not fulfilment, is what the world permits us.

Christopher Fry

Only the first bottle is expensive.

Old French proverb

Intemperance is the physician's provider.

Publius Cyrus

Drunk for 1d, dead drunk for 2d, clean straw for nothing.

Notice outside London gin shops, 1900s

What's so unpleasant about being drunk?
You ask a glass of water.

Douglas Adams, *The Hitchhiker's Guide to the Galaxy*

We don't have a town drunk. We all share the
responsibility.

Anon

When the cock is drunk, he forgets about the
hawk.

Ghanaian proverb

'My country, right or wrong', is a thing no
patriot would think of saying except in a
desperate case. It is like saying, 'My mother,
drunk or sober'.

G. K. Chesterton

When you woo a wet goddess, there's no use
falling at her feet.

W. C. Fields (explaining why he never got falling-down
drunk)

Christmas at my house is always at least six or seven times more pleasant than anywhere else. We start drinking early. And while everyone else is seeing only one Santa Claus, we'll be seeing six or seven.

W. C. Fields

A new telephone survey says that 51 per cent of college students drink until they pass out at least once a month. The other 49 per cent didn't answer the phone.

Craig Kilborn

There are two things that will be believed of any man whatsoever, and one of them is that he has taken to drink.

Booth Tarkington

Of course I'm drunk! What do you think I am? A stunt driver?

Bumper sticker

I'm so drunk my head doesn't even need my neck.

Philip Roth

After I quit drinking, I realised I am the same asshole I always was; I just have fewer dents in my car.

Robin Williams

Ah yes, yes, once in a while indulge ... spree and pee ... look at the girls and a brawl ... not too bloody ... ring around the rosie ... you know ... shake the bugs out of the rug.

Henry Miller

Five stages of drunkeness: Verbose, jocose, lachrymose, bellicose, comatose.

Anon

All right, remember – alcohol equals puke equals smelly mess equals nobody likes you!

'Robbie', *The Wedding Singer*

One swallow does not make a summer but too many swallows make a fall.

George Prentice

And Noah began to be an husbandman, and he planted a vineyard: and he drank of the wine, and was drunken: and he was uncovered within his tent.

Genesis 9:20

I'm very drunk and I intend on getting still drunker before this evening's over.

'Rhett Butler', *Gone with the Wind*

Bring us a pitcher of beer every seven minutes until someone passes out. Then bring one every ten.

'Thornton Melon', *Back to School*

Only promise me one thing, don't take me home until I am drunk . . . very drunk indeed!!

'Holly Golightly', *Breakfast At Tiffany's*

Why don't you stop drinking? Anybody can be a drunk.

'Tully', *Barfly*

Be always drunken. Nothing else matters: that is the only question. If you would not feel the horrible burden of Time weighing on your shoulders and crushing you to the earth, be drunken continually.

Charles Baudelaire

It's the wise man who stays home when he's drunk.

Euripides

In the real dark night of the soul it is always three o'clock in the morning.

F. Scott Fitzgerald

Why is it that to the drunk everything seems to travel in a circle, and that as drunkenness gets more hold men cannot count objects at a distance?

Aristotle

You can be brilliant sometimes, when you're drunk, but brilliance is out of place in the proof-reading department. Dates, fractions, semicolons – these are the things that count. And these are the things that are most difficult to track down when your mind is all ablaze.

Henry Miller

I should like to sit down with half a dozen close companions and drink myself to death but I am sick alike of life, liquor and literature.

F. Scott Fitzgerald

GETTING STRAIGHT

Don't smoke too much, drink too much, eat too much or work too much. We're all on the road to the grave – but there's no need to be in the passing lane.

Robert Orben

I don't do drugs any more … than the average touring funk band.

Bill Hicks

I'm only doing brandy suppositories these days.

Keith Moon

I don't use drugs, my dreams are frightening enough.

M. C. Escher

The talk shows are stuffed full of sufferers who have regained their health – congressmen who suffered through a serious spell of boozing and skirt-chasing, White House aides who were stricken cruelly with overweening ambition, movie stars and baseball players who came down with acute cases of wanting to trash hotel rooms while under the influence of recreational drugs. Most of them have found God, or at least a publisher.

Calvin Trillin

I don't do drugs anymore 'cause I find I get the same effect just by standing up really fast.

Jonathan Katz

I want to give something back. Something that recovery from drugs and alcohol has given me – the chance to live again – with my health – and a better understanding of who I am and what is important in my life.

Eric Clapton

I'll have a dry sherry around noon, maybe a glass of wine at lunch and then in the evening I'll have two or three gin and tonics and half a bottle of wine and probably a couple of brandies, which for me is practically being teetotal.

George Melly

I changed my life. It sounds pretty corny but I kissed drugs goodbye. They were just taking out too much. I was depressed and felt weak and when I talked to a doctor about it he gave me simple but sound advice: Kick the drugs.

Noel Gallagher

My father is my idol, so I always did everything like him. He used to work two jobs and still come home happy every night. He didn't do drugs or drink, and he wouldn't let anyone smoke in his house. Those are rules I adopted, too.

Earvin 'Magic' Johnson

If you want to quit drinking, just look at a drunkard when you're sober.

Chinese proverb

When you stop drinking, you have to deal with this marvellous personality that started you drinking in the first place.

Anon

This is the way I look when I'm sober. It's enough to make a person drink.

Lee Remick

ABSTAINER, *n.* A weak man who yields to the temptation of denying himself a pleasure.

Ambrose Bierce, *The Devil's Dictionary*

My worst day sober is better than my best day drunk.

Anon

If I woke up today feeling like I did every day when I drank, I'd take myself to the emergency room.

Anon

Abstaining is favourable both to the head and the pocket.

Horace Greeley

Complete abstinence is easier than perfect moderation.

Saint Augustine

All philosophy lies in two words, sustain and abstain.

Epictetus

The only way for a rich man to be healthy is by exercise and abstinence, to live as if he were poor.

William Temple

Taking the pledge will not make bad liquor into good, but it will improve it.

Mark Twain

How I do hate those enemies of the human race who go around enslaving God's free people with pledges to quit drinking instead of to quit wanting to drink.

Mark Twain

He shall separate himself from wine and strong drink, and shall drink no vinegar of wine, or vinegar of strong drink, neither shall he drink any liquor of grapes, nor eat moist grapes, or dried.

Numbers 6:3

Drink and the world drinks with you. Swear off and you drink alone.

Anon

Cider, I will not sip, It shall not pass my lip,
Because it has made drunkards by the score.
The Apples I will eat, But cider, hard or sweet,
I will not touch, or taste, or handle more.

19th-century temperance poem

One reason why I don't drink is because I wish to know when I am having a good time.

Nancy Astor

The spirit of the world, the great calm presence of the creator, comes not forth to the sorceries of opium or of wine. The sublime vision comes to the pure and simple soul in a clean and chaste body.

Ralph Waldo Emerson

If you resolve to give up smoking, drinking and loving, you don't actually live longer; it just seems longer.

Clement Freud

I don't drink anymore, but I don't drink any less.

Anon

Recovery is a journey, not a destination.

Anon

I went on a diet, swore off drinking and heavy eating, and in 14 days I lost two weeks.

Joe E. Lewis

If I give up drinking, smoking and fatty foods, I can add ten years to my life. Trouble is, I'll add it to the wrong end.

P. J. O'Rourke

I gave up drinking once – it was the worst afternoon of my entire life.

Humphrey Bogart

There are people who strictly deprive themselves of each and every eatable, drinkable and smokable which has in any way acquired a shady reputation. They pay this price for health. And health is all they get for it. How strange it is. It is like paying out your whole fortune for a cow that has gone dry.

Mark Twain

I felt my heart curl and my scalp hum. Why? I gave up spirits three days ago.

Martin Amis, *Money*

Temperate temperance is best; intemperate temperance injures the cause of temperance.

Mark Twain

The unfortunate thing about this world is that the good habits are much easier to give up than the bad ones.

W. Somerset Maugham

There was once a man who learnt to mind his own business. He went to heaven. I hope teetotallers will remember that.

T. W. H. Crosland

Giving up spirits is OK so long as you drink an incredible amount of beer, sherry, wine and port and can cope with especially bad hangovers.

Martin Amis

Coming of a temperance family, drunkenness
had always been for me a symbol of freedom.

Louis MacNeice

When the pain of staying sober becomes less
than the pain of getting drunk, you'll stay sober.

Anon

You're ready for sobriety when the alcohol
doesn't work anymore.

Anon

I haven't done drugs now for two years, and I
haven't felt this good in my life, ever.

Noel Gallagher

Sobriety is not for people who need it, it's for
people who want it.

Anon

When we were using, we didn't have relation-
ships, we took prisoners and held hostages.

Anon

A sobering thought: what if, at this very
moment, I am.

Jane Wagner

And he that will to bed go sober
Falls with the leaf still in October.

John Fletcher

Sobriety diminishes, discriminates, and says no;
drunkenness expands, unites, and says yes. Not
through mere perversity do men run after it.

William James

How do you look when I'm sober?

Ring Lardner

It would be better that England should be free than that England should be compulsorily sober.

William Connor Magee (speech to House of Lords)

A night sober is a night wasted, but a night wasted is really fun.

Anon

You'd be surprised how much fun you can have sober. When you get the hang of it.

'Joe', *Days of Wine and Roses*

GIN

The proper union of gin and vermouth is a great and sudden glory; it is one of the happiest marriages on earth, and one of the shortest lived.

Bernard De Voto

No man is genuinely happy, married, who has to drink worse gin than he used to drink when he was single.

H. L. Mencken

Gin was mother's milk to her.

'Eliza Doolittle', *Pygmalion*

The shortest way out of Manchester is notoriously a bottle of Gordon's gin.

William Bolitho

Liquid madness sold at tenpence the quartern.

Thomas Carlyle

Gin and drugs, dear lady, gin and drugs.

T. S. Eliot (asked about inspiration)

That humble and much reviled liquid which is the most especially English of all spirits.

William Henry Hazlitt

217

They all thought she was dead; but my father he kept ladling gin down her throat till she came to so sudden that she bit the bowl off the spoon.

'Eliza Doolittle', *Pygmalion*

HANGOVERS

A dusty thudding in his head made the scene before him beat like a pulse. His mouth had been used as a latrine by some small creature of the night and then as its mausoleum.

Kingsley Amis, *Lucky Jim*

Take a hair of the dog that bit you.

Proverb

A hangover is when you open your eyes in the morning and wish you hadn't.

'Andy Capp'

218

I was left in no doubt as to the severity of the hangover when a cat stamped into the room.

P. G. Wodehouse

A hangover is something to fill a head that was empty the night before.

Anon

The hangover became a part of the day as well allowed for as the Spanish siesta.

F. Scott Fitzgerald

A hangover is the wrath of grapes.

Anon

They [hangover cures] omit altogether the psychological, moral, emotional, spiritual aspects: all that vast, vague, awful, shimmering, metaphysical superstructure that makes the hangover a (fortunately) unique route to self-knowledge and self-realisation.

Kingsley Amis

HEROIN

I chose not to choose life, I chose something else. And the reasons? There are no reasons, who needs reasons when you've got heroin?

'Mark Renton', *Trainspotting*

You can never have too many films about Scottish heroin addicts.

Joe Queenan

Junk is the ideal product ... the ultimate merchandise. No sales talk necessary. The client will crawl through a sewer and beg to buy.

William S. Burroughs

In the old days, I really didn't want to deal with being a star every day, and you could kind of hide inside heroin. It was like a cocoon – a soft wall between you and everything else.

Keith Richards

In the heroin business, the Mexicans are the short-order cooks. The French are the chefs.

Sterling Johnson

The needle is not important. Whether you sniff it smoke it eat it or shove it up your ass the result is the same: addiction.

William Burroughs

Who lives longer: the man who takes heroin for two years and dies, or the man who lives on roast beef, water and potatoes till 95? One passes his 24 months in eternity. All the years of the beef-eater are lived only in time.

Aldous Huxley

Dealing Junk:
Never give anything away for nothing. Never give more than you have to give (always catch the buyer hungry and always make him wait). Always take everything back if you possibly can.

William Burroughs

I'll die young, but it's like kissing God.

Lenny Bruce

Heroin – imagine the best orgasm you have ever had and multiply it by a thousand and you're still nowhere near it.

'Mark Renton', *Trainspotting*

Heroin consolidates all your problems into one big one. No more worrying about aggression, repression, poverty, futility and frustration – just heroin, and how to get hold of it.

Joe Axton

The pyramid of junk, one level eating the level below.

William S. Burroughs

It's destructive. It's not beautiful. It is ugly. And this is not about art. It's about life and death. And glorifying death is not good for any society.

Bill Clinton (talking about heroin chic)

Photographers now know if you take heroin-type pictures, it's out of fashion.

Michael Williams, photographer

It's so good. Don't even try it once.

Intravenous heroin user

The arms the Taliban are buying today are paid for with the lives of young British people buying their drugs on British streets. That is another part of their regime that we should seek to destroy.

Tony Blair

In the words of total need: 'Wouldn't you?' Yes, you would. You would lie, cheat, inform on your friends, steal, do anything to satisfy total need … a rabid dog cannot choose but bite.

William S. Burroughs

I was addicted to cocaine until I met Jesus . . . then he introduced me to heroin.

Anon

LSD AND PSYCHEDELICS

Would LSD become a blessing for humanity, or a curse? This I often asked myself when I thought about my problem child.

Albert Hofmann (discoverer of LSD)

I have never recovered from that shattering ontological confrontation. I have never been able to take myself, my mind, and the social world around me seriously.

Timothy Leary (about his first acid trip)

I had not expected that LSD, with its unfathomably uncanny, profound effects, so unlike the character of a recreational drug, would ever find worldwide use as an inebriant.

Albert Hofmann

Psychedelics free us from the anxiety – make us less of a terrified victim and more of a spectator.

Terence Mckenna

There I was, poised in space, a disembodied eye, invisible, incorporeal, seeing but not seen.

R. Gordon Wasson (describing magic mushrooms)

Psychedelia is not just weirder than the drug-naive mind conceives, it's weirder than the drug-naive mind can conceive.

Anon

If you've never seen an elephant ski then you've never been on acid!

Eddie Izzard

If God dropped acid, would he see people?

Stephen Wright

When I see people taking acid to get into my music, I don't want to play that kind of music. I don't want to make people think they've got to use some sort of elevation to get into what I do. If I did that, what kind of artist would I be? Just another phoney asshole.

Captain Beefheart

Going indoors I find that all the household furniture is alive. Everything gestures. Tables are tabling, pots are potting, walls are walling, fixtures are fixturing – a world of events instead of things.

Alan W. Watts

Did the saints owe their visions to some biological short-circuit which caused them to experience spontaneously what LSD cultists achieve with a chemical? Can their mystic raptures be traced to a malfunction of the adrenal glands? Does the faith-state have a neurological basis? Is the religious experience as such nothing more than a fluke of body chemistry?

William Braden

Studying the Human Mind without Psychedelic drugs is like studying religion without a Bible.

Terence Mckenna

Hippies were standing around the streets waiting for the exact appointed minute to strike so they could all publicly swallow their LSD the exact second it became illegal.

Paul Krassner (talking about the day LSD was made illegal)

I wish Bill Gates the best, I really do. I just think he and Microsoft are a bit narrow. He'd be a broader guy if he had dropped acid once or gone off to an ashram when he was younger.

Steve Jobs (Co-founder of Apple Computers)

That's the most acid I've ever seen anyone take. I hope you're not busy for, like, a month.

'Man Stoner', *Up in Smoke*

My previous psychedelic sessions had opened up sensory awareness, pushed consciousness out to the membranes . . . But LSD was something different. It was the most shattering experience of my life.

Timothy Leary

I can't even remember what drug I'm on, but I know it's acid.

Robert F. Campbell

Blinking for an instant I was lost within myself on a path in a garden, which became a forest, which became a world, which became a Universe, and every time I glanced back there was nothing.

Zachary Moser

Then there was LSD, which was supposed to make you think you could fly. I remember it made you think you couldn't stand up, and mostly it was right.

P. J. O'Rourke

LSD melts in your mind, not in your hand.

Anon

Of course, the drug does not produce the transcendent experience. It merely acts as a chemical key – it opens the mind, frees the nervous system of its ordinary patterns and structures. The nature of the experience depends almost entirely on set and setting.

Timothy Leary

It [LSD] went on for years. I must have had a thousand trips. I used to just eat it all the time.

John Lennon

It [LSD] opened my eyes. We only use one-tenth of our brain. Just think of what we could accomplish if we could only tap that hidden part! It would mean a whole new world if the politicians would take LSD. There wouldn't be any more war or poverty or famine.

Paul McCartney

The PC is the LSD of the 1990s.

Timothy Leary

I used to eat it [LSD] like candy.

John Lennon

The central irony of LSD is that it has been used both as a weapon and a sacrament, a mind control drug and a mind-expanding chemical.

Martin A. Lee and Bruce Shlain

A psychedelic is the solvent which dissolves the vigorous stereotypes of egocentric behaviour.

Michael Hollingshead

MARIJUANA

When I was in England, I experimented with marijuana a time or two, and I didn't like it and didn't inhale and never tried it again.

Bill Clinton

As usual, marijuana saves an otherwise disastrous day.

'Pnub', *Idle Hands*

Make the most of the Indian hemp seed, and sow it everywhere!

George Washington

Marijuana is not much more difficult to obtain than beer. The reason for this is that a liquor store selling beer to a minor stands to lose its liquor license. Marijuana salesmen don't have expensive overheads, and so are not easily punished.

William F. Buckley, Jr

A friend with weed, is a friend indeed!

Anon

Weed is not a drug or a bad habit. It is actually a lifestyle.

Anon

If a man wishes to rid himself of a feeling of unbearable oppression, he may have to take hashish.

Friedrich Nietzsche

I now have absolute proof that smoking even one marijuana cigarette is equal in brain damage to being on Bikini Island during an H-bomb blast.

Ronald Reagan

Marijuana is like Coors beer. If you could buy the damn stuff at a Georgia filling station, you'd decide you wouldn't want it.

Billy Carter

Marijuana is ... self-punishing. It makes you acutely sensitive, and in this world, what worse punishment could there be?

P. J. O'Rourke

I tried marijuana, didn't like it particularly and unlike President Clinton I did inhale.

Mo Mowlam

I think smoking grass in junior high school is really a stupid thing to do. Because it seems to me that what you're doing is you're cutting down the sharpness and clarity of the cognitive tools you have to develop a structure for grounding, for effectively functioning within the social structure. And then once you have that, then you can start to develop the other parts of your being.

Richard Alpert (Ram Dass)

I don't respond well to mellow, you know what I mean, I have a tendency to . . . if I get too mellow, I ripen and then rot.

Woody Allen

One's condition on marijuana is always existential. One can feel the importance of each moment and how it is changing one.

Norman Mailer

Is marijuana addictive? Yes, in the sense that most of the really pleasant things in life are worth endlessly repeating.

Richard Neville

I not only think joints should be legalised, I think it should be mandatory! That would be a nice world, wouldn't it? Quiet, mellow, hungry, high people everywhere. Highways filled with nothing but 'Domino's Pizza' trucks.

Bill Hicks

Aaah, they lie about marijuana: tell you pot-smoking makes you unmotivated. Lie. When you're high, you can do everything you normally do, just as well, you just realise it's not worth the f**king effort.

Bill Hicks

I don't know, I never smoked Astroturf.

> Frank Edwin 'Tug' McGraw, New York Mets (asked
> whether he preferred artificial turf or grass)

If marijuana is a dangerous drug, the greatest danger associated with smoking it may lie in being arrested.

> Robert M. Julien

God made pot… Man made beer… Who do you trust?

> Katie Santo

If god had meant for us not to fly, he wouldn't have given us marijuana.

> Patrick Marlowe

While it is undoubtedly the case that many drug addicts started with cannabis, to claim that taking cannabis is bound to lead to hard drugs has always seemed to me far-fetched.

> Jack Straw, *Daily Telegraph*

235

We consider it undesirable to prosecute genuine therapeutic users of cannabis who possess or grow cannabis for their own use. This unsatisfactory situation underlines the need to legalise cannabis preparations for therapeutic use.

House of Lords, Great Britain, 'Therapeutic Uses of Cannabis' Select Committee on Science and Technology, 14 March, 2001

No one knows, when he places a marijuana cigarette to his lips, whether he will become a joyous reveller in a musical heaven, a mad insensate, a calm philosopher, or a murderer.

Harry J. Anslinger, Commissioner of the US Bureau of Narcotics 1930–62

The drug is really quite a remarkably safe one for humans, although it is really quite a dangerous one for mice and they should not use it.

J. W. D. Henderson, Director of the Bureau of Human Drugs, Health and Welfare, Canada

Marijuana inflames the erotic impulses and leads to revolting sex crimes.

Daily Mirror (1924)

I advise any bashful young man to take hashish when he wants to offer his heart to any fair lady, for it will give him the courage of a hero, the eloquence of a poet, and the ardour of an Italian.

'Dr Meredith' in Louisa May Alcott's *Perilous Play*

When you return to this mundane sphere from your visionary world, you would seem to leave a Neapolitan spring for a Lapland winter – to quit paradise for earth – heaven for hell! Taste the hashish, guest of mine – taste the hashish!

Alexandre Dumas, *The Count of Monte Cristo*

[A marijuana taker] will suddenly turn with murderous violence upon whomever is nearest to him.

American Journal of Nursing, 1936

Hippies, hippies . . . they want to save the world but all they do is smoke pot and play frisbee!

'Eric Cartman', South Park

Marijuana will be legal some day, because the many law students who now smoke pot will someday become congressmen and legalise it in order to protect themselves.

Lenny Bruce

MARTINI

FRASIER: Y'know, Niles, what say I buy us dinner and a lot of martinis?
NILES: Sounds great, except for the dinner part.

Frasier

I am prepared to believe that a dry martini slightly impairs the palate, but think what it does for the soul.

Alec Waugh

A martini is like a woman's breast. One ain't enough and three is too many.

'Cocktail waitress', *The Parallax View*

I must get out of these wet clothes and into a dry Martini.

Alexander Woollcott

A medium vodka dry Martini – with a slice of lemon peel. Shaken and not stirred.

Ian Fleming, *Dr No*

The martini, once a symbol of American imbibing, memorialised in thousands of neon outlines of cocktail glasses, is becoming an amusing antique, like a downtown art deco apartment building.

J. D. Reed

Well, all right, but it is cold on the stomach.

Joseph Stalin (accepting a martini mixed by Franklin D. Roosevelt at a Soviet-US meeting)

You can no more keep a martini in the refrigerator than you can keep a kiss there. The proper union of gin and vermouth is a great and sudden glory; it is one of the happiest marriages on earth, and one of the shortest-lived.

Bernard Devoto

He was white and shaken, like a dry martini.

P. G. Wodehouse (describing a startled Englishman)

The three-martini lunch is the epitome of American efficiency. Where else can you get an earful, a bellyful and a snootful at the same time?

Gerald R. Ford

All my life I've been terrible at remembering people's names. I once introduced a friend of mine as Martini. Her name was actually Olive.

Tallulah Bankhead (explaining why she calls everybody 'dahling')

240

A well-made Martini or Gibson, correctly
chilled and nicely served, has been more often
my true friend than any two-legged creature.

M. F. K. Fisher

Happiness is a good martini, a good meal, a
good cigar and a good woman ... or a bad
woman, depending on how much happiness you
can stand.

G. K. Chesterton

For a Cannibal Martini, take 1/3 vermouth, 2/3
gin, and into this drop a small girl named Olive.

Fred Allen

FATIMA BLUSH: Oh, how reckless of me. I've
made you all wet.
JAMES BOND: Yes, but my Martini's still dry.

Ian Fleming, *Never Say Never Again*

OPIUM

Everything one does in life, even love, occurs in an express train racing toward death. To smoke opium is to get out of the train while it is still moving. It is to concern oneself with something other than life or death.

Jean Cocteau

Tobacco and opium have broad backs, and will cheerfully carry the load of armies, if you choose to make them pay high for such joy as they give and such harm as they do.

Ralph Waldo Emerson

Thou hast the keys of Paradise, oh just, subtle, and mighty opium!

Thomas De Quincey , *Confessions of an Opium Eater*

It is not opium which makes me work but its absence, and in order for me to feel its absence it must from time to time be present.

Antonin Artaud

The smell of opium is the least stupid smell in the world.

Pablo Picasso

Among the remedies which it has pleased Almighty God to give to man to relieve his sufferings, none is so universal and so efficacious as opium.

Thomas Sydenham

There is no Turk who would not buy opium with his last penny.

Belon (sixteenth-century French naturalist)

The death of ennui is the most efficient bribe which opium offers.

Silas Weir Mitchell

It banishes melancholy, begets confidence, converts fear into boldness, makes the coward eloquent, and dastards brave.

John Brown, *Elementis Medicinae* (1780)

One must not think life with the mind, but with opium.

André Malraux

Opium teaches only one thing, which is that aside from physical suffering, there is nothing real.

André Malraux

Nobody will laugh long who deals much with opium: its pleasures even are of a grave and solemn complexion.

Thomas De Quincey

PIPE SMOKING

Pipe smokers spend so much time cleaning, filling and fooling with their pipes, they don't have time to get into mischief.

Bill Vaughan

May my last breath be drawn through a pipe, and exhaled in a jest.

Charles Lamb

I believe that pipe smoking contributes to a somewhat calm and objective judgement in all human affairs.

Albert Einstein

Nowhere in the world will such a brotherly feeling of confidence be experienced as amongst those who sit together smoking their pipes.

Dr. Barnstein, *The Results and Merits of Tobacco* (1844)

The fact is, squire, the moment a man takes to a pipe, he becomes a philosopher. It's the poor man's friend; it calms the mind, soothes the temper, and makes a man patient under difficulties. It has made more good men, good husbands, kind masters, indulgent fathers, than any other blessed thing on this universal earth."

Thomas Chandler Haliburton, *The Clockmaker*

There is no composing draught like the draught through the tube of a pipe.

Captain Frederick Marryat

A pipe is the fountain of contemplation, the source of pleasure, the companion of the wise; and the man who smokes, thinks like a philosopher and acts like a Samaritan.

E. G. Bulwer-Lytton

A pipe is to the troubled soul what caresses of a mother are for her suffering child.

Indian proverb

Pipe smoking is the most protracted of all forms of tobacco consumption. It may explain why pipe smokers are generally regarded as patient men – and philosophers.

Jerome E. Brooks

There is no more harm in a pipe than in a cup of tea. You may poison yourself by drinking too much green tea, and kill yourself by eating too many beefsteaks. For my part, I consider that tobacco, in moderation, is a sweetener and equaliser of the temper.

Thomas Henry Huxley

The pipe draws wisdom from the lips of the philosopher, and shuts up the mouth of the foolish; it generates a style of conversation, contemplative, thoughtful, benevolent, and unaffected.

William Makepeace Thackeray

Pipe smoking is properly an intellectual exercise.

Christopher Morley

A Dutchman without a pipe is a national impossibility. If a Dutchman were deprived of his pipe and tobacco, he would not even enter Paradise with a glad heart.

Schotel

Smoke. Smoke. Smoke. Only a pipe distinguishes man from beast.

Honoré Daumier

UYU have proved it is a very moral habit.

Benjamin Disraeli to Colonel Webster

A pipe in the mouth makes it clear that there has been no mistake – you are undoubtedly a man.

A. A. Milne

PORT

Port is not for the very young, the vain and the active. It is the comfort of age and the companion of the scholar and the philosopher.

Evelyn Waugh

It is my opinion that nothing seasons the mind for endurance like hard work. Port wine should perhaps be added.

Anthony Trollope

I have often thought that the aim of port is to give you a good and durable hangover, so that during the next day you should be reminded of the splendid occasion the night before.

George Mikes

Port is the wine proper to the heavy drinker.

Evelyn Waugh

The heavy port drinker must be prepared to make some sacrifice of personal beauty and agility.

Evelyn Waugh

I only drink fortified wines during bad weather. Snowstorm, hurricane, tornado – I'm not particular, as long as it's bad. After all, any storm for a Port.

Paul S. Winalski

PUBS

A good local pub has much in common with a church, except that a pub is warmer, and there's more conversation.

William Blake

A bartender is just a pharmacist with a limited inventory.

Anon

If anyone knows of a pub that has draught stout, open fires, cheap meals, a garden, mother-ly barmaids and no radio, I should be glad to hear of it, even though its name were something as prosaic as the Red Lion or the Railway Arms.

George Orwell

A tavern is a place where madness is sold by the bottle.

Jonathan Swift

So, you hate your job? Join our support group: it's called EVERYBODY! They meet at the bar.

Drew Carey

The easiest way to spot a wanker in a pub is to look around and find who's drinking a Corona with a slice of lemon in the neck.

Warwick Franks

Sometimes, you hit the bar, and sometimes, the bar hits you.

Jeffrey Lebowski

Good puzzle would be to cross Dublin without passing a pub.

James Joyce

The pub, with its elaborate social ritual, its animated conversations and – at any rate in the North of England – its songs and weekend comedians, is gradually replaced by the passive, drug-like pleasures of the cinema and the radio.

George Orwell

TEA

Now then Father, what would you say to a nice cup of tea?

'Mrs Doyle', *Father Ted*

It's the best tea. It's Indian tea, of course. We may be at war with India, but there's no reason to overreact.

'Major Rasul', *Vertical Limit*

Thank God for tea! What would the world do without tea? How did it exist? I am glad I was not born before tea.

Sydney Smith

Why do they always put mud into coffee on board steamers? Why does the tea generally taste of boiled boots?

William Makepeace Thackeray

Is there any tea on this spaceship?

'Arthur Dent', *The Hitchhiker's Guide to the Galaxy*

Free yourselves from the slavery of tea and coffee and other slopkettle.

William Cobbett, *Advice to Young Men*

Our trouble is that we drink too much tea. I see in this the slow revenge of the Orient, which has diverted the Yellow River down our throats.

J. B. Priestley

Is there no Latin word for 'tea'? Upon my soul, if I had known that I would have let the vulgar stuff alone.

Hilaire Belloc

Love and scandal are the best sweeteners of tea.

Henry Fielding, *Love in Several Masques*

We live in stirring times – tea-stirring times.

Christopher Isherwood

A woman is like a tea bag: She does not know how strong she is until she is in hot water.

Nancy Reagan

I'd much rather have a good cup of tea than sex.

Boy George

No matter how rushed your schedule is, spend at least five minutes in the morning quietly in bed with your loved one just being gentle together. Perhaps drinking tea.

Michael Ventura

Tea with us became more than an idealisation of the form of drinking; it is a religion of the art of life.

Kakuzo Okakura, *The Book of Tea*

The Way of Tea lies in studying the ceremony, in understanding the principles, and in grasping the reality of things. These are its three rules.

Hosokawa Tadaoki

Drink your tea slowly and reverently, as if it is the axis on which the earth revolves – slowly, evenly, without rushing toward the future. Live the actual moment. Only this moment is life.

Thich Nat Hahn

When the world is falling apart around you,
drink tea.

Anon

Tea is such a magical product – perhaps even
the eighth wonder of the world.

Mr H. Rahman, Senior Tea Buyer at Harrods

Oh don't you know, I'm the new tea lady round
here.

Mo Mowlam (to Bill Clinton, after being cold-shouldered
by Tony Blair, at a meeting with the US President)

You have arrived at a propitious moment [Mr
Bond], coincident with your country's one
indisputable contribution to Western civilisation
– afternoon tea.

'Hugo Drax', *Moonraker*

I am in no way interested in immortality, but
only in the taste of tea.

Lu T'ung

Throughout the whole of England the drinking of tea is general. You have it twice a day and though the expense is considerable, the humblest peasant has his tea, just like the rich man.

La Rochefoucauld

All well-regulated families set apart an hour every morning for tea and bread and butter.

Joseph Addison

The British have an umbilical cord which has never been cut and through which tea flows constantly.

Marlene Dietrich

The trouble with tea is that originally it was quite a good drink. So a group of the most eminent British scientists put their heads together, and made complicated biological experiments to find a way of spoiling it. To the eternal glory of British science their labour bore fruit.

George Mikes

As a rule they [the English people] will refuse even to sample a foreign dish, they regard such things as garlic and olive oil with disgust, life is unliveable to them unless they have tea and puddings.

George Orwell

Nobody can teach you how to make the perfect cup of tea. It just happens over time. Wearing cashmere helps, of course.

Jill Dupleix

Where there's tea there's hope.

Arthur Wing Pinero

Ecstasy is a glass full of tea and a piece of sugar in the mouth.

Aleksandr Pushkin

The mere chink of cups and saucers turns the mind to happy repose.

George Gissie

Kissing is like drinking tea with a tea strainer, you can never get enough.

Anon

It has been well said that tea is suggestive of a thousand wants, from which spring the decencies and luxuries of civilisations.

Agnes Repplier

VODKA

Vodka and Coca-Cola. Detente in a glass!

Vernon Bayliss, *Defence of the Realm*

We need to open another bottle of vodka. It seems that you put most of the last bottle in your mouth.

'Chap', *The Daytrippers*

I used to drink vodka and tonics all the time, but I found my kidneys got really hard because of it and I noticed that my liver wouldn't drop down in my yoga back bends.

Gwyneth Paltrow

There's no absolutes in life – only vodka.

Mick Jagger

And God said, 'Let there be vodka!'
And He saw that it was good.
Then God said, 'Let there be light!'
And then He said, 'Whoa – too much light'.

Anon

Vodka is our enemy, so let's finish it off.

Russian proverb

There's only one bottle of vodka left. I don't know what to do.

Peter the Great

Who keeps the tavern and serves up the drinks?
The peasant. Who squanders and drinks up
money belonging to the peasant commune, the
school, the church? The peasant. Who would
steal from his neighbour, commit arson and
falsely denounce another for a bottle of vodka?
The peasant.

Anton Chekhov

If I only had enough vodka for two men and
enough women for four, I would lead a very
happy life.

Anon

WHISKY

I love to sing and I love to drink scotch. Most
people would rather hear me drink scotch.

G. K. Chesterton

Find out what whisky he drinks and send all of my generals a case, if it will get the same results.

Abraham Lincoln (in reply to comments about General Grant's drinking problems)

When you work hard all day with your head and know you must work again the next day what else can change your ideas and make them run on a different plane like whisky?

Ernest Hemingway

A man can take a little bourbon without getting drunk, but if you hold his mouth open and pour in a quart, he's going to get sick on it.

Lyndon Johnson

I'm for anything that gets you through the night, be it prayer, tranquillisers or a bottle of Jack Daniels.

Frank Sinatra

If alcohol is the crutch, then Jack Daniels is a wheelchair.

Anon

They say some of my stars drink whisky, but I have found that ones who drink milkshakes don't win many ball games.

Casey Stengel

God invented whisky so the Irish wouldn't rule the world!

Anon

A torchlight procession marching down your throat.

John Louis O'Sullivan

Love makes the world go round? Not at all. Whisky makes it go round twice as fast.

Compton Mackenzie

Whisky is by far the most popular of all remedies that won't cure a cold.

Jerry Vale

Whisky is for drinking; water is for fighting over.

Mark Twain

Freedom and Whisky gang thegither!

Robert Burns

There aren't many left like him nowadays, what with education and whisky the price it is.

Evelyn Waugh

How well I remember my first encounter with The Devil's Brew. I happened to stumble across a case of bourbon – and went right on stumbling for several days thereafter.

W. C. Fields

A good gulp of hot whisky at bedtime – it's not very scientific, but it helps [to cure a cold].

Alexander Fleming

Whisky is what makes a man shoot at his landlord and miss.

Irish proverb

Have respect for age. Drink good scotch.

Anon

You can't even order a shot of whisky anymore without some special little story being attached to it.

Denis Leary

Whisky and vermouth cannot meet as friends, and the Manhattan is an offence against piety.

Bernard De Voto

Philosophising while partially embalmed in whisky never does produce much more than a whining little tribe of clichés.

Keri Hulme

Scotch Whisky to a Scotchman is as innocent as milk is to the rest of the human race.

Mark Twain

There is nothing like whisky in this world for preserving a man when he is dead; but it is one of the worst things in the world for preserving a man when he is living.

Dr Guthrie, *The Temperance Handbook*

An old stomach reforms more whisky drinkers than a new resolve.

Don Marquis

WINE

I'd rather have a case of the clap than a case of this wine.

'Vince', *Cousins*

Hey Man, I'm drinking wine, eating cheese and catching some rays.

'Oddball', *Kelly's Heroes*

I like to drink wine more than I used to. Anyway, I'm drinking more.

'Vito Corleone', *The Godfather*

Wine makes old wives wenches.

John Clarke

Good wine carrieth a man to heaven.

Anglo-Saxon proverb

Frenchmen drink wine just like we used to drink water before Prohibition.

Ring Lardner

And Noah he often said to his wife when he sat down to dine, 'I don't care where the water goes if it doesn't get into the wine.'

G. K. Chesterton, 'Wine and Water'

Food without wine is a corpse; wine without food is a ghost; united and well matched they are as body and soul, living partners.

André Simon

In water one sees one's own face; but in wine, one beholds the heart of another.

Old French proverb

Never refuse wine. It is an odd but universally held opinion that anyone who doesn't drink must be an alcoholic.

P. J. O'Rourke

My books are water; those of the great geniuses are wine. Fortunately, everybody drinks water.

Mark Twain

Fish, to taste good, must swim three times: in water, in butter, and in wine.

Polish proverb

If you see in your wine the reflection of a person not in your range of vision, don't drink it.

Chinese proverb

I love your lips when they're wet with wine and red with a wicked desire.

Ella Wheeler Wilcox, 'I Love You'

If food is the body of good living, wine is its soul.

Clifton Fadiman

My friends should drink a dozen of claret on my Tomb.

John Keats

It is wrong to do what everyone else does – namely, to hold the wine list just out of sight, look for the second cheapest claret on the list, and say, 'Number 22, please'.

Stephen Potter

Wine and cheese are ageless companions, like aspirin and aches, or June and moon, or good people and noble ventures.

M. F. K. Fisher

Wine should be taken in small doses; knowledge in large ones.

Chinese proverb

Wine is a mocker, strong drink a brawler, and whoever is led astray by it is not wise.

Proverbs 20:1

So the Lord awakened as one out of sleep: and like a giant refreshed with wine.

Psalm 78:3

Men are like a fine wine. They all start out like grapes, and it's our job to stomp on them and keep them in the dark until they mature into something which you'd like to have dinner with.

Anon

Wine is like sex in that few men will admit not knowing everything about it.

Hugh Johnson

Drinking wine is not a snobbism nor a sign of sophistication, nor a cult; it is as natural as eating and to me as necessary.

Ernest Hemingway

Red wine with fish. Well, that should have told me something.

Ian Fleming, *From Russia with Love*

271

Wine hath drowned more people than the sea.

Anon

What I like to drink most is wine that belongs to others.

Diogenes

Sorrow can be alleviated by good sleep, a bath and a glass of wine.

Thomas Aquinas

One of the penalties of being president of the United States is that you must subsist for four years without drinking anything except Californian wine.

A. J. P. Taylor

This wine is too good for toast-drinking, my dear. You don't want to mix emotions up with a wine like that. You lose the taste.

Ernest Hemingway

272

Wine makes a man better pleased with himself.
I do not say that it makes him more pleasing to
others . . . This is one of the disadvantages of
wine, it makes a man mistake words for
thoughts.

Samuel Johnson

Wine gives a man nothing. It neither gives him
knowledge nor wit; it only animates a man, and
enables him to bring out what a dread of the
company has repressed. It only puts in motion
what had been locked up in frost.

Samuel Johnson

If you are poor, avoid wine as a costly luxury; if
you are rich, shun it as a fatal indulgence. Stick
to plain water.

Herman Melville

Quickly, bring me a beaker of wine, that I may
wet my brain and say something clever.

Aristophanes

Give me books, fruit, French wine and fine weather and a little music out of doors, played by someone I do not know . . . I admire lolling on a lawn by a water-lilied pond to eat white currants and see goldfish: and go to the fair in the evening if I'm good. There is not hope for that – one is sure to get into some mess before evening.

John Keats

Good or bad, it is my country's wine.

Chinese proverb

A meal without wine is like a day without sunshine.

Louis Pasteur

Wine does not intoxicate men; men intoxicate themselves.

Chinese proverb

Wine is the milk of old age.

Sir William Osler

The great evil of wine is that it first seizes the feet, it is a crafty wrestler.

Plautus

I can certainly see that you know your wine. Most of the guests who stay here wouldn't know the difference between Bordeaux and Claret.

Basil Fawlty

Wine is a peep-hole on a man.

Alcaeus

Despair is vinegar from the wine of hope.

Austin O'Malley

I rather like bad wine . . . one gets so bored with good wine.

Benjamin Disraeli

If God forbade drinking, would He have made wine so good?

Cardinal Richelieu

Drink to me only with thine eyes,
And I will pledge with mine;
Or leave a kiss but in the cup
And I'll not look for wine.

Ben Jonson

There is not the hundredth part of the wine
consumed in this kingdom that there ought to
be. Our foggy climate wants help.

Jane Austen, Northanger Abbey

Burgundy for kings, champagne for duchesses,
claret for gentlemen.

French proverb

The best use of bad wine is to drive away poor
relations.

French proverb

In vino veritas.

Pliny The Elder

Drink wine, and you will sleep well. Sleep, and you will not sin. Avoid sin, and you will be saved. Ergo, drink wine and be saved.

Medieval German saying

One not only drinks wine, one smells it, observes it, tastes it, sips it, and one talks about it.

King Edward VII

Beer is made by men, Wine by God.

Martin Luther

A barrel of wine can work more miracles than a church full of saints.

Italian proverb

Wine is bottled poetry.

Robert Louis Stevenson

What is better than to sit at the end of a day and drink wine with friends, or substitute for friends.

James Joyce

What is life to a man deprived of wine?

Ecclesiastes

Wine is the remedy for the moroseness of old age.

Plato

Wine is sunlight held together by water.

Galileo

Wine improves with age. The older I get, the better I like it.

Raymond George

The more specific the name, the better the wine.

Frank Schoonmaker

A hard drinker, being at table, was offered grapes at dessert. 'Thank you,' said he, pushing the dish away from him, 'but I am not in the habit of taking my wine in pills.'

Anthelme Brillat-Savarin

To buy very good wine nowadays requires only money. To serve it to your guests is a sign of fatigue.

William F. Buckley

From behind the red gates comes the stink of wine and meat, while along the roadsides lie the bones of the frozen dead.

Chinese proverb

Dinner possessed only two dramatic features – the wine was a farce and the food a tragedy.

Anthony Poole

Lords are lordliest in their wine.

John Milton

It is widely held that too much wine will dull a man's desire. Indeed it will – in a dull man.

John Osborne

Hide our ignorance as we will, an evening of wine soon reveals it.

Heraclitus

Americans are rather like bad Bulgarian wine: they don't travel well.

Bernard Falk

Tis pity wine should be so deleterious,
For tea and coffee leave us much more serious.

Lord Byron

Wine is the drink of the gods, milk the drink of babes, tea the drink of women, and water the drink of beasts.

John Stuart Blackie

Wine is a living liquid containing no preservatives. Its life cycle comprises youth, maturity, old age, and death. When not treated with reasonable respect it will sicken and die.

Julia Child

Who hath woe? Who hath sorrow? Who hath contentions? Who hath babblings? Who hath wounds without cause? Who hath redness of eyes? They that tarry long at the wine; they that go to seek mixed wine.

Proverbs 23:29–30

I have enjoyed great health at a great age because every day since I can remember I have consumed a bottle of wine except when I have not felt well. Then I have consumed two bottles.

Bishop of Seville

One that hath wine as a chain about his wits, such a one lives no life at all.

Alcaeus

Drink no longer water, but use a little wine for thy stomach's sake.

New Testament, 1 Timothy 5 v. 23

It is better to hide ignorance, but it is hard to do this when we relax over wine.

Heraclitus

Wine gives courage and makes men more apt for passion.

Ovid

Strategy is buying a bottle of fine wine when you take a lady out for dinner. Tactics is getting her to drink it.

Frank Muir

There is nothing like good food, good wine, and a bad girl.

Anon

The wine seems to be very closed-in and seems to have entered a dumb stage. Sort of a Marcel Meursault.

Paul S. Winalski

Religions change; beer and wine remain.

Hervey Allen

What grape, to keep its place in the sun, taught our ancestors to make wine?

Cyril Connolly

Conversation is the enemy of good wine and food.

Alfred Hitchcock

Wine has made me bold but not foolish; has induced me to say silly things but not to do them.

Duff Cooper

What is man, when you come to think upon him, but a minutely set, ingenious machine for turning with infinite artfulness, the red wine of Shiraz into urine?

Isak Dinesen (Karen Blixen)

What contemptible scoundrel stole the cork from my lunch?

W. C. Fields

Wine makes daily living easier, less hurried, with fewer tensions and more tolerance.

Benjamin Franklin

Wine is the most civilised thing in the world.

Ernest Hemingway

Wine can of their wits the wise beguile, Make the sage frolic, and the serious smile.

Homer

I have trodden the wine-press alone.

Isaiah 63:3

What is the definition of a good wine? It should start and end with a smile.

William Sokolin

Droplets of rain can soak through your clothes; goblets of wine can wash away your wealth.

Chinese proverb

Nothing equals the joy of the drinker, except the joy of the wine in being drunk.

French proverb

God made only water, but man made wine.

Victor Hugo

It is a maudlin and indecent verity that comes out through the strength of wine.

Joseph Conrad

Great people talk about ideas, average people talk about things, and small people talk about wine.

Fran Lebowitz

Fan the sinking flame of hilarity with the wing of friendship; and pass the rosy wine.

Charles Dickens, *The Old Curiosity Shop*

Let him kiss me with the kisses of his mouth! For your love is better than wine.

Song of Solomon 1:2

I edit out the bad stuff and deliver the good stuff. Seventy-five per cent of all wine is awful.

Peter Morrell, vintner

I have lived temperately … I double the doctor's recommendation of a glass and a half of wine a day and even treble it with a friend.

Thomas Jefferson

Good wine needs neither bush nor preface to make it welcome.

Sir Walter Scott

The First Duty of wine is to be Red . . . the second is to be a Burgundy.

Harry Waugh

Come, come, good wine is a good familiar creature if it be well used; exclaim no more against it.

William Shakespeare, *Othello*

For a bad night, a mattress of wine.

Spanish proverb

Wine is valued by its price, not its flavour.

Anthony Trollope

When wine is spilled with accident, death and disaster hasten.

Joseph O'Donnell

And no one puts new wine into old wineskins; otherwise, the wine will burst the skins, and the wine is lost, and so are the skins; but one puts new wine into fresh wineskins.

Mark 2:22

Music and Wine are one.

Ralph Waldo Emerson

Water for oxen, wine for kings.

Spanish proverb

If you have wine today, get drunk today; worry about tomorrow's worries tomorrow.

Chinese proverb

He who has wine and meat will have many friends.

Chinese proverb

Do not look at wine when it is red, when it sparkles in the cup and goes down smoothly. At the last it bites like a serpent, and stings like an adder. Your eyes will see strange things, and your mind utter perverse things. You will be like one who lies down in the midst of the sea, like one who lies on the top of a mast. 'They struck me,' you will say, 'but I was not hurt; they beat me, but I did not feel it. When shall I awake? I will seek another drink'.

Proverbs 23:31–5

A bottle of wine begs to be shared; I have never met a miserly wine lover.

Clifton Fadiman

Excellent wine generates enthusiasm. And whatever you do with enthusiasm is generally successful.

Philippe de Rothschild

There is evil in every berry of grape.

The Koran

The scent of wine, oh how much more
agreeable, laughing, praying, celestial and
delicious it is than that of oil!

François Rabelais

To take wine into our mouths is to savour a
droplet of the river of human history.

Clifton Fadiman

I drank a bottle of wine for company. It was
Chateau Margaux. It was pleasant to be
drinking slowly and to be tasting the wine and
to be drinking alone. A bottle of wine was good
company.

Ernest Hemingway

Wine is made to be drunk as women are made
to be loved; profit by the freshness of youth or
the splendor of maturity; do not await
decrepitude.

Theophile Malvezin

There can be no bargain without wine.

Latin proverb

You have only so many bottles in your life, never drink a bad one.

Len Evans

The discovery of a wine is of greater moment than the discovery of a constellation. The universe is too full of stars.

Benjamin Franklin

Wine makes every meal an occasion, every table more elegant, every day more civilised.

André Simon

If you have more pleasure in the taste of wine than in the use of your sight, wine is good for you; but if the pleasure of seeing be greater to you than that of drinking, wine is naught.

John Locke

The good talk that is inseparable from a wine dinner is even more important than the wines that are being served. Never bring up your better bottles if you are entertaining a man who cannot talk. Keep your treasures for a night when those few who are nearest to your heart can gather round your table, free from care, with latchkeys in their pockets and no last train to catch.

Maurice Healy

A mind of the calibre of mine cannot derive its nutriment from cows.

George Bernard Shaw

If we sip the wine, we find dreams coming upon us
Out of the imminent night

D. H. Lawrence, 'Grapes'

Drink a glass of wine after your soup and you steal a ruble from your doctor.

Russian proverb

If you wish to grow thinner, diminish your dinner,
And take to light claret instead of pale ale.

Henry Leigh

I made wine out of raisins so I wouldn't have to wait for it to age.

Steven Wright

The juice of the grape is the liquid quintessence of concentrated sunbeams.

Thomas Love Peacock

By making this wine vine known to the public, I have rendered my country as great a service as if I had enabled it to pay back the national debt.

Thomas Jefferson

Every cask smells of the wine it contained.

Spanish proverb

Wine is the best broom for troubles.

Japanese proverb

Boys should abstain from all use of wine until their 18th year, for it is wrong to add fire to fire.

Aristotle

I sat at a table where were rich food and wine in abundance, and obsequious attendance, but sincerity and truth were not; and I went away hungry from the inhospitable board.

Henry David Thoreau

A man may surely be allowed to take a glass of wine by his own fireside.

Richard Brinsley Sheridan (drinking a glass of wine in the street and watching his theatre, the Drury Lane, burn down)

The Wine of Life keeps oozing drop by drop,
The Leaves of Life keep falling one by one.

> Edward Fitzgerald, *The Rubaiyat of Omar Khayyam*

Wine is felt by the French nation to be a
possession which is its very own, just like its
three hundred and sixty types of cheese and its
culture.

> Roland Barthes

He that drinks wine drinks blood, and he that
drinks water drinks phlegm.

> John Florio

In the order named these are the hardest to
control: Wine, Women, and Song.

> Franklin P. Adams

So far round the twist you could use him to
open wine bottles.

> Terry Pratchett, *Wyrd Sisters*

Wine prepares the heart for love, unless you take too much.

Ovid

Wine is like rain: when it falls on the mire it but makes it the fouler,
But when it strikes the good soil wakes it to beauty and bloom.

John Hay

And what wine is so sparkling, what so fragrant, what so intoxicating, as possibility!

Soren Kierkegaard

Deep colour and big shaggy nose... That genuine extract from a wine journal is the sort of thing that gets the stuff a bad name.

Kingsley Amis

Shew not thy valiantness in wine; for wine hath destroyed many.

Ecclesiastes 34:25–31

Sake starts out as a friend, but can end as an enemy.

Japanese proverb

Too much and too little wine. Give him none, he cannot find truth; give him too much, the same.

Blaise Pascal

Wine exalts the will; hashish destroys it. Wine is a physical stimulant; hashish a suicidal weapon. Wine mellows us and makes us sociable; hashish isolates us.

Charles Baudelaire

Index

HIGH SOCIETY